One-Day Retreats for Senior High Youth

One-Day Retreats for Senior High Youth

Geri Braden-Whartenby and
Joan Finn Connelly

Saint Mary's Press
Christian Brothers Publications
Winona, Minnesota

Love and thanks to our husbands and children:
Bill Braden-Whartenby and Dylan
Tom Connelly, Megan and Matthew

Authors' Acknowledgments

We wish to thank the Sisters of Charity of Convent Station for having a vision of retreat ministry and a dedication to it. We especially thank Sister Carol Heller, SC, director of Xavier Retreat and Conference Center, for giving us the encouragement and freedom to create the retreats. We are most grateful for her confidence in us and the gift she has for drawing out the best in people. We also thank Marianne Kehoe, program director, for sharing her ideas and for allowing us to use her as a sounding board for our concepts and activities. Thanks to Margaret Clark for proofreading our work. Thanks to all the members of the staff of Xavier Center who make working there a joy and a privilege.

Thanks also to the thousands of teens who have come on retreat with us and shared their faith with us. This certainly has kept us motivated. We especially thank Sacred Heart Youth Group, Lyndhurst, New Jersey, Saint Mary's Youth Group, Dumont, New Jersey, and Saint Thomas Youth Group, Bloomfield, New Jersey.

And we wish to thank the adults, both professionals and volunteers, who work with teens. The adults' dedication to the teens and their faith development has been an inspiration for us.

 Genuine recycled paper with 10% post-consumer waste. Printed with soy-based ink.

The cross design on the cover is by Robert Palladino. Used with permission of Printery House of Conception Abbey, Conception, Missouri.

The publishing team for this book included Robert P. Stamschror, development editor; Rebecca Fairbank, copy editor; Barbara Bartelson, production editor and typesetter; Kent Linder, cover designer; Maurine R. Twait, art director; pre-press, printing, and binding by the graphics division of Saint Mary's Press.

The acknowledgments continue on page 141.

Printed in the United States of America

Printing: 9 8 7 6 5 4 3 2 1

Year: 2005 04 03 02 01 00 99 98 97

ISBN 0-88489-369-3

Contents

Introduction   7

Retreat 1: Celebrating Diversity   14

Retreat 2: Graduation   31

Retreat 3: Peacemaking   51

Retreat 4: Prayer and Our Relationship with Jesus   72

Retreat 5: Self-Esteem   96

Retreat 6: Sexuality   112

Appendix
  A. Icebreakers   129
  B. Guided Meditations Tips   137
  C. Muscle Relaxation Exercises   137
  D. Tips for Small-Group Facilitators   139

Introduction

Who We Are   Let us introduce ourselves. We are Geri Braden-Whartenby and Joan Finn Connelly. Each of us is Roman Catholic with a master's degree in religious education from La Salle University, Philadelphia, and a graduate certificate in youth ministry. Geri has been a parish youth minister, a campus minister, and a parish director of religious education. She is now the director of youth services for Xavier Retreat and Conference Center in Convent Station, New Jersey. Joan has been a parish youth minister and a high school religion teacher. She is now the associate youth retreat director at Xavier Center. We each have fourteen years' experience. Together we direct over one hundred retreats a year, and we also do retreat training, and communication and conflict resolution training for adults and teens.

Our Kind of Retreat   Our retreat philosophy incorporates active-learning exercises, a sound biblical foundation, and meaningful prayer experiences. Evaluations returned to us by adult moderators of youth groups have affirmed our philosophy.

Active learning simply means "learning by doing." In our retreats we hope to reach our objectives by having teens use their senses in a variety of ways. Active learning keeps young teens moving, knowing that they will remember much more of what they do than what they hear. A study cited in a 1995 issue of *Group* magazine reports that we remember 20 percent of what we read, 30 percent of what we hear, 40 percent of what we see, 50 percent of what we say, 60 percent of what we do, and 90 percent of what we see, hear, say, and do (p. 16).

Active learning is not all fun and games. It takes more preparation than a lecture and requires more faith and trust because the adult is not controlling the learning by feeding information, but instead is allowing the Holy Spirit to work, through the activities, in the teens themselves. With active learning you are never quite sure of the results. But if it is done well, active learning provides valuable lessons more effectively than does a more rote style of learning.

The Bible is filled with stories of active-learning experiences, each requiring trust that learners would "catch on"—for example, the stories of Abraham and Isaac, Jonah, and Noah and the flood. In Jesus we have a great teacher to follow because he used active learning strategies throughout his life. The storm on the lake, the woman caught in adultery, and the washing of the disciples' feet are examples. It was a pretty risky teaching style, but if God can risk active learning, maybe we can too.

Another part of our retreat philosophy is providing teens with a strong biblical foundation. Each retreat incorporates time for reflection on the Scriptures. Retreatants have the opportunity to read a passage from the Scriptures, reflect on its meaning, and see how the lessons from the passage connect with their personal growth and faith journey. Providing teens with a strong biblical foundation fosters a more mature faith formation.

Each retreat begins and ends with prayer. The opening prayer sets the tone for the day. It creates an environment that encourages teens to be open to God's spirit at work in them. The concluding prayer, a guided meditation, allows teens to listen to God, something that tends to be neglected in their fast-paced lives.

Retreat Overview

Theme The theme provides the retreat director with a concise purpose for the day.

Bible Basis The Scripture cite for the message that the combined retreat activities intend to communicate is provided. The Scripture passage both supports the theme of the retreat and serves as the inspiration for creating and selecting the retreat activities. It is also hoped that the teens will come away from the retreat with an appreciation for the richness and guidance the Scriptures provide for their daily life.

Objectives The objectives expand on the theme and provide specific learning outcomes for the retreat.

Retreat at a Glance This chart is offered at the beginning of each retreat plan. It gives the director an overview of the retreat, including the time frames and materials needed for each activity.

Retreat in Detail This section of the retreat plan contains the bulk of the retreat resources. It gives detailed directions for carrying out the activities of the retreat that are listed in the Retreat at a Glance chart. The retreats vary in length but typically run about six hours, and never exceed seven hours. All the retreats include the following elements:

Welcome and Introduction

A spirit of hospitality is conveyed to the teens in the welcome and introduction. If the retreat director does not know the group, this is a good time to start building a rapport with them. In this introduction the retreat director may do one or more of the following tasks:
• Convey appreciation to the teens for taking the time to participate in the retreat.

- Share a personal story from a retreat experience and explain how it affected him or her.
- Explain the significance of a retreat. For example, we tell teens that a retreat is time away from their normal routine to reflect on their life, experience new things, quiet themselves down to be open to God's spirit, pray, enjoy being with their friends, and learn about others.
- Highlight the philosophy of a retreat.
- Communicate the housekeeping information and rules. For example:
  - Give directions to the bathrooms and other facilities.
  - Explain regulations regarding smoking.
  - Offer an explanation of what rooms in the building are available for their use and what areas outside are designated for recreation at lunchtime.
- Go over the retreat theme and schedule. Retreats are not intended to be mystery games. Informing the teens of the retreat theme and schedule demonstrates respect. Most teens are open to whatever you have planned.

  On occasion we have led retreats in which after going over the theme and schedule, the teens said they had already done some of the planned exercises. Sometimes they wanted to do them again, and sometimes they preferred to do something different. Giving the teens some say in the retreat prompts a readiness to participate and a willingness to try new experiences.
- Present the retreat standards. Teens usually come to a retreat with a variety of prior retreat experiences and levels of openness. During the greeting convey that the day will be filled with fun and learn–ing, but along with fun comes some rules. (We call them *standards* rather than rules because teens often have a negative reaction to the word *rules*.) These standards try to anticipate the usual things some teens will do to try to disrupt the retreat (thus heading them off at the pass).

  Standards that we recommended include:
  - What's said here, stays here.
  - Only one person speaks at a time.
  - Put-downs, both verbal and physical, are off-limits.
  - Questions are welcomed.
  - You may decline when invited to share.
  - Be open and try.

  Establishing standards right away gives structure and bound-aries to the teens. The boundaries allow them to see that "anything does *not* go" on this retreat. Some young people come because they have to and therefore may express some resentment and resistance. Some come expecting not to participate. The standards clarify ac-ceptable and unacceptable behavior during the retreat.

  After going over the standards, ask the participants if they would like to add any standards to make the day go smoothly. Then direct them to nod if they find the standards reasonable and are willing to abide by them. Post the standards in a place where they can serve as a reminder during the retreat of what the group has agreed on.

Holding the teens accountable to the standards is important. If a standard is violated, acknowledge the violation and its consequences, and remind the young people that they agreed to follow the standards. If this is not done, the standards will not mean anything to the retreatants.

Icebreakers

Icebreakers are important. Part A of the appendix offers several to choose from, or you can use your own. Icebreakers conducted at the beginning of the retreat are meant to help relax the young people, show them that the retreat is meant to be fun as well as spiritual, and get them accustomed to working in small groups. Icebreakers conducted immediately following lunch are meant to bridge the transition between the unstructured lunchtime and the structured program. These games help the teens refocus and re-enter the spirit of the retreat.

The following guidelines will help to enhance the effectiveness of icebreakers:
- Practice them ahead of time to ensure you have all the necessary materials and are able to give clear directions.
- Have some large-group icebreakers and then some small-group ones.
- Do not use icebreakers that might embarrass some retreatants.
- Do not continue to play the games over and over. They are meant to be introductory.
- Do not be afraid to try the same icebreaker again with a new group if the first group did not like it or if it did not go well the first time. For example, we often start our retreats with the icebreaker People Upset (see part A of the appendix). It is a great large-group game that gets teens running around and intermingling. The game involves different people winding up as leader in the center of the circle. We played the game with a group we did not know well, and one teen stood in the center of the circle. We waited for him to make the next move, but he did not. A teacher quickly came over and told us that the young man was a new resident of the United States and did not speak English. We respectfully invited him back to the group and assigned another teen to continue the game. If that had been our first experience with People Upset, we may never have used it again. Not all icebreakers work with all groups. If one occasionally does not work, it may not be the icebreaker but the makeup of the group.

Opening Prayer

Simple opening prayers are provided for each retreat. They may be read aloud by the teens or by the retreat director. You may want to add a song, or you may want to allow time for individual petitions, knowing that "where two or three are gathered in Christ's name, there he is."

Retreat Activities

A variety of activities flesh out each retreat. These include personal reflection exercises and small- and large-group activities. You may wish to keep the same small groups throughout the retreat or to form new groups for each small-group activity. That is up to you. All the instructions needed to carry out the activities are included. Each activity builds on the previous one. The retreats usually start with light, simple activities. As the day progresses, the activities become more challenging. Therefore, we encourage you to use the activities in the order presented.

Affirmation

Going through adolescence is a tough experience. Teens need to know that they are loved for who they are and who they are becoming. Statistics show that from sixth grade to twelfth grade a young person's self-image typically decreases. There are many reasons for this: media portrayals of the ideal person, biological changes going on inside the teenager, attraction to the other sex, and the added stress of more responsibility.

Unfortunately teens focus on negative images of themselves rather than on positive ones. To compensate for this, affirmation is built in throughout the retreats, and one specific affirmation activity is placed near the end of each retreat so that the teens can leave with positive feelings.

Closing Guided Meditation

Many teens have told us that they really like guided meditations. They say that these experiences provide some of the few opportunities they have to relax and really pray. After one guided meditation, a young man said that he really liked it. When asked why, he responded, "My father has been dead awhile, and during the meditation I got to speak with him one more time."

Concluding each retreat with a guided meditation not only gives teens this quiet time to be with God but also shows them that God is truly present in their life.

Progressive Muscle Relaxation

Starting a guided meditation with progressive muscle relaxation allows the teens to calm themselves down enough to be open to the guided meditation. Several progressive muscle relaxation exercises are given in part C of the appendix.

Evaluation

Evaluation helps teens reflect on the whole retreat and what it has meant to them. A simple way to do this is to ask these three questions:
• If you had only one word to describe today, what one word would you pick?

- What is one new thing you learned today, or what is one thing that you really liked?
- What do you feel God is challenging you to do as a result of this retreat?

Helpful Hints

We have found the following strategies to be useful in making the retreat run smoothly:

- When teens are in small groups working on an assignment, alert them to the time remaining with 5-minute, 2-minute, and 1-minute signals. This helps them pace themselves so that they will not be surprised or upset when time is called.
- In some of the retreat activities, we assign teens to be leaders by calling out a certain quality or criterion, such as, "those whose birthday is closest to Christmas," or "the person with the longest name." A variety of measures like these increases the likelihood that during the retreat many young people will have the opportunity to be a leader.
- During break time the retreatants may choose to eat a snack. We inform them before they take their break to finish all food or drink before returning to the meeting area. Having teens eating and drinking during the retreat activities is not only distracting for them but for the retreat director as well.
- Be prepared. Gather all needed materials before the retreat. If the retreat director appears unprepared, the teens will know it. Time spent finding things disrupts the flow of the retreat and loses the teens' attention.
- The material in this book is geared for groups of up to thirty-five participants, with the whole group often being separated into small groups. The ideal small-group size is six to eight participants. Because significant small-group activity is part of the retreat, we encourage you to used trained small-group facilitators. Trained facilitators will enhance the retreat experience for the teens. (See part D of the appendix for a list of tips you can provide to facilitators.) Facilitators can be older high school students, teachers, parents, catechists, or other volunteers. Facilitators are especially helpful for younger teens who may or may not be used to working together.

Debriefing Activities

Most of the retreat activities end with questions that can be used to discuss the meaning of that particular exercise. As alternatives to posing the questions to the large group and having volunteers answer, you could do the following:

- Have the teens return to their small groups and discuss the questions. Then invite each small-group leader to report back to the large group.
- Assign different questions to each small group and have the small-group leaders report back to the large group.

• Decide as a group on a one-sentence moral to the exercise. Present the moral or message in a creative fashion, such as a song, a bumper sticker, or a mime.

Competition Versus Cooperation

The directions for some of our icebreakers and retreat activities suggest telling the group that the first team finished "wins." We certainly want teens to feel good about themselves throughout the retreat, and not to be put in the position of being "losers." However, teens in the United States are used to competing, and many are motivated by rewards. The icebreakers and some of the small-group activities that appear to be competitive in nature actually challenge the teens to cooperate as a team within small groups and to engage only in mini-competition with other small groups.

We give prizes to winning teams only when doing so is necessary to the activity. When prizes are not required, we tell winning teams who ask what their reward or prize is, "You win our deepest appreciation and congratulations." At the end of each game or performance-type activity, we applaud those who participated.

Some groups need to be motivated initially by some form of competition. If you feel that your group does not need the added motivation that competition provides, simply give instructions for the groups to accomplish the activity, and call time when they appear to be finished.

We usually remark at some point in the retreat that we enjoyed many games that did not involve declaring a winner. We try to help the young people realize that participating in an activity and working cooperatively with their team members is more important than winning.

Our Hope

Retreats have proven to be valuable and effective in the faith formation of teens. We hope that the retreats in this book prove to be an effective tool to help bring your group to a deeper faith.

Retreat 1

Celebrating Diversity

Theme   This retreat addresses the issues that underlie racism and explores ways to diminish the negative effects of racism.

Bible Basis   *Col. 3:10–14.* Saint Paul reminds us that all people are equal in God's eyes. Therefore, we are to treat everyone with love, compassion, gentleness, and mercy.

Objectives   The retreatants will do the following:
- define prejudice, stereotype, racism, and diversity
- examine the tendency in society to blame the victim
- appreciate their own and others' ethnic and cultural background
- reflect on the Gospel value of unconditional love
- practice ways to reduce prejudice

Retreat at a Glance

The following chart offers a brief overview of the retreat activities, time frames, and materials needed. For more detailed information about any of the activities, refer to the directions given in the Retreat in Detail section.

ACTIVITY	TIME FRAME	SUPPLIES
Welcome and Introduction	10–15 minutes	poster with standards
Icebreakers	15–30 minutes	depends on selection
Opening Prayer	5 minutes	Bible
20/20 Vision	10 minutes	numbered cards with images
Wagon Wheel	10–15 minutes	
Culture Cake	15–25 minutes	handout 1–A, pencils, Bible
Pick Your Corner	10 minutes	
Break	10 minutes	
Universal Quality	10–15 minutes	poster with quote
Gift Giving	20–25 minutes	newsprint, marker, scrap paper, pencils, poster with names of people, poster with gifts, Bible
Labels That Limit	10–15 minutes	newsprint, marker, scrap paper, pencils
Lunch	45 minutes	
Icebreakers	15 minutes	depends on selection
Can I Get In?	15–20 minutes	newsprint, marker, Bible
Billings' Victory Over Hate	15 minutes	
Cooperative Line Crossing	10 minutes	masking tape
Diversify Yourself	20–30 minutes	newsprint, marker
What Others Think of Me	15–20 minutes	paper, pencils
Closing Guided Meditation	20–30 minutes	instrumental music, tape or CD player
Evaluation	5 minutes	pencils, paper

Retreat in Detail

Welcome and Introduction

(10–15 minutes)

Icebreakers

(15–30 minutes)

Choose from among the icebreakers offered in part A of the appendix of this book, or use games of your own.

Opening Prayer

(5 minutes)

Begin the prayer by reading Col. 3:10–14—Paul's instruction on God's universal love.

Finish with a prayer similar to this one:

- Dear God, Saint Paul reminds us that everyone is included in your family. Yet we know that our families, schools, neighborhoods, and even our world are torn apart by prejudice and racism. We ask for the grace today
  - to see people as you see them
  - to be forgiven for the times we have judged or hurt others because of our own prejudices and fear
  - to heal us for the times we have been victims of hatred
  - to strengthen us to show love in the face of hatred and fear

  God, you have graced us with the gift of diversity. All we have to do is look around at creation to see the beauty and harmony that diversity provides. Increase our sympathy, compassion, and understanding. Let us continue to appreciate all the gifts you have given us and all the gifts we see in others. May we live in unity and peace. Amen.

20/20 Vision

Large-Group Activity (10 minutes)

This activity helps the teens realize that not everyone sees things the same way, even when looking at the same object or situation.

Recreate the images below on numbered cards or sheets of paper large enough so that they can be seen by all when held up in front of the group. Possible interpretations of each image are listed below the image:

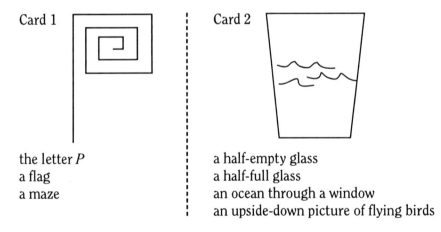

Card 1

the letter *P*
a flag
a maze

Card 2

a half-empty glass
a half-full glass
an ocean through a window
an upside-down picture of flying birds

Card 3

a foot buried in the sand
gravestones
teeth

Card 4

a sunrise over mountains
a sunset over mountains
a waffle ice-cream cone
a spider

Card 5

GODISNOWHERE

God is nowhere
God is now here
God I snow here (for the skiers!)

Show the group all the illustrations and ask volunteers to state what they see in each image. Then pose these questions to the whole group:

- Why didn't we all see the same thing in each image?
- Who interpreted the images correctly?
- What would we need to do in order for others to see an image the way we see it?

Offer a conclusion like this to the activity:

- This activity demonstrates that we all have perceptions about things. Our perception of an object, a scene, an event, or even a person will not always be the same as someone else's. We all see differently because we are all unique. Being unique is a God-given gift. Unfortunately in our society, differences are often looked at as something bad rather than as something to rejoice about.

Wagon Wheel **Large-Group Activity (10–15 minutes)**
In this activity the teens get to know one another better and share their experiences of diversity.

Have everyone stand. Divide the group in half. Direct one half to form a circle facing outward. Direct the other half to form a circle around the first circle, facing in.

Give these directions in your own words:

- You now face your first partner. I am going to read a question, and you are to share your answer with your partner. After you both have answered, I am going to call "Rotate," and the outer circle is to move one person to the right so that everyone has a new partner. Then I will read another question for you and your new partner to answer.

Read the following questions one at a time. Direct the outer circle to rotate after each question:

- What's the best place you have ever visited?
- What is one nice thing about you?

- How many members are in your family?
- Where were you born?
- What is your favorite food for lunch?
- What does your family like to do together?
- What does your family usually cook for Christmas?
- What is your favorite ethnic food?
- When did you first realize you are different from everyone else?
- Did you ever witness prejudice in action? If so, what did you do?
- Were you ever a victim of prejudice? If so, describe the experience.
- Who has modeled acceptance of others for you?
- What prejudices were you taught?

Feel free to add questions of your own. Continue this activity for 10 minutes or so. Conclude by leading a discussion of the following questions:
- How did it feel to answer these questions?
- Do you now feel a little better acquainted with one another?

Culture Cake

Small-Group Activity (15–25 minutes)

This activity encourages appreciation of the rich diversity among cultures.

1. Form small groups and give each person a pencil and a copy of handout 1–A, "Culture Cake." Offer instructions similar to the following:
- In the past you may have heard the term *melting pot* used in reference to the United States. That term was used early in the twentieth century when many immigrants were coming to this country and melting all together, in other words, becoming assimilated. Unfortunately when we melt together with others we can lose some of our individuality. Today many people use the term *salad bowl* or *culture cake* to describe U.S. culture. I prefer culture cake because each layer of the cake is special and unique and blends well together without melting or losing its original flavor.

    In front of you is a piece of culture cake. Write your first name in the icing at the top, and also write something about how you got your name. Then complete the rest of the handout for your ethnic or racial group. You will get a chance to share your answers with your small group in a few minutes. Please complete the handout in silence.

2. Give everyone enough time to complete the handout. Then offer the small groups these directions:
- You will need a group leader for your discussion. The leader begins the discussion and takes notes on some of the things your group members share. Let's have the person in each group with the longest last name be the leader. The leader first shares his or her name and any history surrounding that name. Then the leader lets everyone else share about their name. Next, the leader shares the ethnic or racial group to which he or she belongs, and then goes around the circle until everyone has shared about that layer of the cake. Continue in the same fashion until everyone has shared all their responses.

3. After the groups are finished, ask the leaders:
- Did anything that was shared in your group surprise you or other members of your small group?
- Which elements of the culture cake prompted the most discussion and sharing?
- Do you think the ethnic or racial status of the members of your group likely influences how they view themselves?

4. Call for a volunteer to read aloud Matt. 5:43–47. Conclude the activity by asking the whole group the following discussion questions (see the introduction for alternative ways of debriefing this and other retreat activities):
- What makes it easy or difficult to be nice to people whom we do not know?
- Are the people you hang around with similar to you or different from you?
- What type of love is Jesus calling us to demonstrate?
- What makes another person or group your enemy? your friend?
- If you love those who love you, what reward do you get?
- If you hate those who hate you, what reward do you get?
- How do Jesus' teachings speak to the way our society deals with social issues such as legal cases, divorce, war, and so on?

Pick Your Corner

Large-Group Activity (10 minutes)
This activity helps the teens realize that we are all a part of several different groups; some we choose to participate in, and others we are born into. The teens also see that appreciating the differences among groups can help us to break down harmful barriers.

1. Designate one corner of the room as the belonging corner, another as the not-belonging corner. Have the retreatants stand, and instruct them by saying something like this:
- When I say the name of a particular group, those who belong to that group should go to the designated corner. Those who do not belong should go to the opposite corner.

  Repeat the procedure with several group names. Possible group names are girls, not girls; tall, not tall; bike riders, not bike riders; Italian, not Italian; only child, not an only child; born in the United States, not born in the United States; multilingual, not multilingual. The pairs of groups you name can be as controversial or noncontroversial as you wish, depending in part on the maturity of the group.

2. Next, ask the whole group these questions:
- What is a group?
- What are some of the groups you belong to?
- Which groups were you born into? Which did you join?
- Why are we part of groups? What are the rewards of belonging to groups?
- What are some of the disadvantages of belonging to groups?

3. Conclude the activity by using words similar to the following:
- We all belong to many groups, some by choice and some by birth. Staying only with the people who are like us can isolate us from the

rich experiences others have to share with us and can also make us afraid of others. Understanding the differences among groups can help us to appreciate the gifts each brings to humanity.

(Based on Kreidler, *Creative Conflict Resolution*, p. 162)

Break (10 minutes)

Universal Quality Large-Group Activity (10–15 minutes)

Through this activity the retreatants come to appreciate that diversity is a universal quality.

Write the following quote from the French philosopher Montaigne on a sheet of newsprint:

- There never was in the world two opinions alike,
  No more than two hairs or two grains.
  The most universal quality is diversity.

Have a volunteer read the quote. Then raise the following discussion questions:

- What does *diversity* mean? What does *universal* mean?
- What is Montaigne saying in this quote? Do you agree with him?
- In what ways is diversity good? In what ways might it be bad?
- What effect might diversity have on conflicts between people?
- How do you respond to people who are like you? somewhat different from you? very different from you?

(Based on Kreidler, *Creative Conflict Resolution*, p. 156)

Conclude the activity by expressing the following thoughts in your own words:

- God created diversity throughout nature. We read in Genesis how God created everything and then looked at it and called it "good." Diversity is essential. Just think about how our world functions. It is dependent on many different types of plants, animals, and insects to make a complete, functioning ecosystem. So, too, human communities benefit from a variety of cultures, races, religions, and ethnic groups. Try to imagine what life would be like if we all looked, acted, talked, dressed, and thought the same way? What if all restaurants served only hot dogs and hamburgers, or we only had apples for a snack? It would get pretty boring after awhile. Diversity makes life interesting. Unfortunately, racial, ethnic, and religious discrimination are commonplace in this country and around the world. Although dealing with this topic can be difficult, it is vital, for the future of our society, to address it so that different cultures and countries can live and work peacefully together.

Gift Giving Small-Group Activity (20–25 minutes)

This activity introduces the term *prejudice.*

Before the retreat, write the following definition of prejudice on newsprint:

- Prejudice is an unfavorable opinion or feeling formed about something or someone without knowledge, thought, or reason.

Prepare the two posters needed in step 2.

1. Form small groups. Begin the activity by conveying the following ideas in your own words:
- The very simple task I am about to give you measures your ability to make judgments based on very limited information. Christmas is approaching, and you have a few last-minute gifts to buy. Choose the most appropriate gift for each of the following people from the options provided. Money is no object, but you can give only one of each gift. Each group needs a recorder to write down the group's decisions and then share them aloud when everyone is done. Let's have the recorder be the oldest person in each group. Any questions?

     Give each group scrap paper and pencils for writing their responses.

2. Hang up the following two posters and read them aloud:
- *Poster 1: People to Buy For*
    - Gertrude: sixty-five years old, has five grandchildren, has been widowed for two years
    - Tony: thirty years old, truck driver, has driven a truck for three years
    - Peter: eleventh-grade student, top of his class in math
    - Chris: thirty-five years old, bank teller for the past three years, single parent
    - Sandy: forty-five years old, teacher of English
- *Poster 2: Gifts to Choose From*
    - A. Book on computer programming
    - B. Set of cushions
    - C. Makeup kit
    - D. Calculator
    - E. Two season tickets to the theater

3. After the students have completed the task, survey the small groups to record the number of groups that selected gift C for Gertrude, B for Tony, A for Peter, D for Chris, and E for Sandy.

4. Lead a discussion with the whole group based on the following questions:
- What thoughts did you have about each person, and how did this affect your choice of gift?
- Why did you make the choices you did?

5. Continue by expressing these ideas in your own words:
- Gertrude may be a senior citizen, but she likes to live in the mainstream. She travels, tries new foods, and has a new computer in her den at home. She would enjoy a new book on computer programming.

     Antoinette (her friends call her Tony) is a student and drives a truck to pay her way through school. A calculator would have been a good choice for a gift.

     Peter is a good student, but studies are not his only interest. He is a member of a clown troupe and is learning how to do clown makeup. A makeup kit would have been a perfect gift for him.

     Chris would have been delighted to receive the theater tickets so that he and his twelve-year-old son could see some plays together. It's hard to make ends meet on Chris's salary, so they don't get out much.

Santiago (Sandy for short) would have loved to receive the set of cushions. After a hard day at work, his favorite pastime is to sit and read or listen to music. He is always glad to put his feet up for a while.

Give the young people a chance to comment.

6. Next, ask:
• What assumptions did you make about the people for whom you chose gifts?

Then say something like this:
• Making assumptions and prejudging situations is something we all do. Sometimes prejudices can be harmful and can block us from seeing other important things about people or situations.

Hang up the poster with the definition of prejudice on it. Invite a volunteer to read aloud Rom. 14:5–11.

7. Conclude the activity by leading a large-group discussion of these questions:
• What does this Scripture passage say about judging others?
• How do you feel when someone misjudges you?
• What can we each do to stop ourselves from judging others?

(Adapted from Huntly, *Rich World, Poor World,* pp. 219, 223)

Labels That Limit

Small-Group Activity (10–15 minutes)

This activity introduces the term *stereotype.*

Prior to the retreat, write this definition of stereotype on newsprint:
• A stereotype is a general viewpoint about a group of people that is not based in fact.

1. Introduce the activity this way:
• Jesus and the Scriptures call us to see people in ways we haven't seen them before. Often when we think of those who are rich, poor, imprisoned, sick, or in any way different from us, we judge them to be better than we are or less than we are. We tend to think of people who are different from us in terms of stereotypes; that is, we put them into a category and label them in a negative way. We don't really see them as individuals. Followers of Jesus are challenged to see people as unique and precious individuals.

Ask the whole group the following question:
• Who in the Scriptures was stereotyped and later befriended by Jesus? [Some examples are his disciples as fishermen, the Pharisees, Zacchaeus, women.]

2. Explain these instructions to the small groups:
• I'm going to read aloud several different categories of people and give you one stereotype about each category. As a small group, you are to write down two more stereotypes for each category. Each group needs a leader who will make sure everyone's ideas are heard. The leader records the group's decisions and then shares them aloud when everyone is done. Let's have the leader be the youngest person in each group. Any questions?

Give each small group scrap paper and pencils for writing its responses.
- List two stereotypes of the poor. [They don't want to work.]
- List two stereotypes of undocumented immigrants. [They take jobs from U.S. citizens.]
- List two stereotypes of prisoners. [They will commit the same crimes again.]
- List two stereotypes of the elderly. [They drive too slowly.]

After naming each category, invite the leaders to share examples of the stereotypes their group wrote.

3. At the end of the activity, pose the following discussion questions to the whole group:
- Where do stereotypes come from?
- What makes them believable or unbelievable?
- Why is it unchristian to stereotype people?

4. Display the definition of *stereotype* and ask if anyone has any questions about it. Give the small groups these directions:
- In your small group, discuss one way you might help people break the pattern of stereotyping others. Then have your group leader share your idea aloud.

Lunch (45 minutes)

Icebreakers (15 minutes)
Choose from among the icebreakers offered in part A of the appendix of this book, or use games of your own.

Can I Get In? Large-Group Activity (15–20 minutes)
The purpose of this activity is to introduce the term *racism*.

Before the activity, write the following definition of the word *racism* on newsprint:
- Racism is the oppression of racial groups; one group has control over another group. Racism combines prejudice with the abuse of power. Although prejudice can be directed toward any group, racism is usually directed toward less-powerful groups and is intended to keep them relatively powerless. Apartheid in South Africa was a manifestation of racism as was slavery in the United States.

1. Have the whole group stand and form a circle. Call for a volunteer to stand outside the circle. Give the following instructions:
- In this activity everyone except a single volunteer stands in a circle. The people in the circle are to hold hands and try to keep the volunteer from getting inside the circle. The volunteer who is on the outside of the circle must do whatever he or she can to get into the center of the circle.

Play the game until either the volunteer gets into the center of the circle or a couple of minutes have passed. Repeat with another volunteer.

2. After the game, invite the teens to sit down. Post the definition of racism and read it aloud to the group. Lead a discussion of the following questions:
- Outsider, how do you feel now? How did it feel being on the outside of the circle?
- Insiders, how did it feel being in the circle?
- What strategies did the outsider use to try to get into the circle? [List these on newsprint.]
- Did any of you insiders feel badly for the outsider? How, if at all, did you act on those feelings? What did you tell yourself that convinced you to keep the outsider out?
- Did the people in the circle talk to one another? If so, about what? If not, why not?

3. Continue the discussion with these comments and questions:
- Now let's compare what happened in the activity to what happens in society.
- Who are some of the more powerful groups of people in our society?
- Which groups are outsiders?
- In society the circle might represent access to power, privileges, jobs, money, and so on. How are some of the strategies the outsider used (or might have used) like the strategies members of minority groups in society use to try to gain opportunities?

4. Further the discussion by expressing the following ideas in your own words:
- In this activity the outsider could have asked politely; used an assertive strategy like giving the group a "talking to" or crawling between legs; been creative—for example, tickling people in the circle; or used force to try to break the insiders' hands apart.

   Many societal comparisons can be drawn. If a girl wanted to be in an all boys' baseball league, she might use a variety of approaches to get in: ask, petition, get so good they want her to play, stage a sit-in on the baseball field.

   During the civil rights movement in this country, black people originally asked for equal rights and later used assertive tactics, including mass marches and freedom rides, to gain national publicity.

5. Ask a volunteer to read Col. 3:10–14. After the reading make this comment:
- Saint Paul reminds us that everyone is included in God's family.
Then ask:
- In what ways is this passage relevant to our discussion?
- What holds people together in society?
- What do the Scriptures say holds people together?
- Let's focus on the majority of people who form the circle:
  - How do people with power and privilege in society keep that power and privilege from others?
  - What arguments do they use? How is this similar to what you did in this activity?
  - What's the advantage to holding on to power? the disadvantage?

(Adapted from Schniedewind and Davidson, *Open Minds to Equality*, pp. 139–140)

Billings' Victory Over Hate

Large-Group Activity (15 minutes)

Read aloud the following story, taken from *USA Weekend:*

- Like a willow in the wind, the people of Billings, Mont., bend, not break. Racial and religious intolerance seems only to make the community stronger. Make A Difference Day 1994 reinforced that unity.

  To understand what happened in Billings, you need some context: In 1992, rocks were thrown through the windows of homes displaying menorahs for Hanukkah. Incensed, 10,000 people put candles in their own windows to show support for the 100 Jewish residents. News of the city's reaction so moved two St. Paul, Minnesota, grade school classes that they raised $720 selling candy to replace the broken windows.

  "We need to speak up for each other," says Tom Polanski, 13, whose class in Minnesota helped victims of anti-Semitism in Montana.

  Two years later, some of the $720 bought paint for Make A Difference, *USA Weekend's* annual national day of community service. That day, 60 Catholics, Jews, Lutherans, Mormons and others united to paint and re-side Wayman African Methodist Episcopal Chapel, the crumbling home of a tiny black congregation. Fewer than half of 1 percent of Billings' 80,000 people are black. A grateful Rev. Bob Freeman, 80, says it seems the nearby railroad tracks no longer split the city racially. Other contributors to the project: anonymous private donors, the Billings Human Rights Foundation and local businesses.

  The volunteers' mood was one of brotherhood, recalls Mayor Richard Larsen. "It shouldn't matter who your neighbor is. We have more people who see that now." (*USA Weekend,* 17–19 March 1995, p. 20)

Afterward lead a discussion with the whole group based on the following questions:

- What were some of the risks people faced by buying candles to put in their own windows to show support for the Jewish families?
- What were the rewards of their efforts?
- How can volunteer service efforts help to dissolve prejudices?
- Does anyone wish to share a story of how others acted against intolerance?
- What are some problems in your own city or school? What can you do to help?

Cooperative Line Crossing

Large-Group Activity (10 minutes)

In this activity the teens realize the benefits of cooperation.

Mark a line down the center of the room with masking tape. Have the teens pair up, with one person on one side of the tape and the other on the opposite side of the tape, facing each other. Then give the following directions:

- The object of the game is to get your partner to cross over the line to your side. Any questions? [The objective is for both teens to agree to cross over the line at the same time. Most likely teens will use force or bribery, like they did in the Can I Get In? activity.]

After the activity ask the whole group:
- Why did you automatically compete?
- What was the goal of the game?
- Did the other person's crossing over to your side mean you lost?
- What did you stand to gain by cooperation?
- Are there other situations in which we compete without thinking?
- What does this game say about being peacemakers?
- Can you cite examples of when Jesus used cooperation rather than competition to deal with a dilemma? [the multiplication of the loaves and fishes]

Conclude the activity by making the following comment in your own words:
- In these last two exercises, you might have thought: "I like being on the inside, it feels good"; "The outsider might feel bad, but it's only a game"; "Winning is everything, whether I get a prize or not."

Diversify Yourself

Small-Group Role-Plays (20–30 minutes)

This activity teaches the retreatants various ways to diversify themselves.

1. List on newsprint the following tips on how to become more aware of the effects of prejudice in your life. Share the corresponding commentaries with the group.
- *Learn to respect yourself.* If you feel good about yourself and your accomplishments, you won't have to put others down to feel good. Realize your value in the community and your potential to make a positive impact.
- *Be open to people and situations you encounter that may not be familiar to you.* Respect new experiences, even if you don't understand them at first.
- *Be proud of your heritage.* Learn to speak your native language, do ethnic dances, tell stories from your culture's history, cook traditional foods. Help others understand that heritage.
- *Learn about other cultures.* If ignorance breeds contempt, awareness breeds acceptance. Celebrate cultural differences as well as similarities. Get to know people from other cultures; you will see that we share many of the same goals, values, and dreams. Almost all teens enjoy music, movies, sports, having fun. You can always find common ground.
- *Learn to identify attitudes and behaviors that lead to discrimination.* Understand your perceptions about people of other races or ethnic groups. Where did these attitudes come from—your family, your friends, the media?
- *Realize that we are responsible for our attitudes and actions and that we have the power to change them.* We must all take responsibility for correcting negative stereotypes that have been created by society and are being passed on to others. Don't be afraid to tell your friends that you don't appreciate hearing negative comments about different groups.

- *Avoid extremist groups that preach hatred toward others.* People are more alike than they are different. We all share the same basic needs.
- *Follow the Golden Rule.* Treat others as you would like to be treated.

2. Next, form small groups. Give each small group a scene to discuss and design a role-play around it. Here are some possible role-play scenes:
- Your friend says he doesn't want to go to a certain shopping mall because too many blacks shop there.
- A friend puts down a Muslim girl because she always wear a scarf.
- You want to talk to a girl you met in math class, but she's talking to two other girls in Spanish, and you don't understand the language.
- At a school dance, you are asked to dance by a girl or boy who is Vietnamese American, and you are a Euro-American.
- You are a team captain for a touch football game in gym class. It's your turn to pick your last player, and three people are left: an African American, a Euro-American, and an Asian American. You've never seen any of them play football.

    Direct the groups to decide on an ending to their scene in which they reduce prejudice. Invite them to perform their role-plays.

3. After each role-play, ask the performing group these questions:
- What did you learn from doing your role-play?
- How did you decide on the ending for your role-play?

4. Conclude the activity by asking the whole group the following questions:
- How might the victim in each role-play feel?
- Would this happen in real life? If so, how?
- What else could be done in this situation?

    (Adapted from Club Connect, Race Relations Kit)

What Others Think of Me

Bob Black

Affirmation (15–20 minutes)

In this activity the teens learn how others see them.

Give everyone a long sheet of paper, 3-by-8 inches or so, and instruct them to write their name at the bottom and a one-word self-description at the top.

Then have them fold the paper down from the top twice in order to conceal their descriptive word. The paper should look like the example in the margin.

Now have the teens exchange sheets two or three times so that they lose track of their own paper. Direct each teen to write, at the top of the paper he or she was given, a one-word description of the person named at the bottom. Tell the teens not to unfold the sheet and look at the person's own self-description.

Ask the teens to be honest, constructive, and as positive as possible about the person they are describing. (If they don't know the person at all, they should leave the paper blank.) The top of the sheet should again be folded down before the sheets are exchanged for another round. Repeat the process until the sheets are full of one-word descriptions of the teen named at the bottom.

When the teens get their own sheet back, give them a few minutes to unfold it and look over their list. Then ask them if anyone wrote the same one-word description that they wrote for themselves. Or invite them to share a description that surprised them.

(Adapted from Rice, *Up Close and Personal*, p. 91)

Closing Guided Meditation

(20–30 minutes)

Begin the meditation with a progressive muscle relaxation exercise (see part C of the appendix for suggestions). If possible, play soft instrumental background music. Then continue with the following guided meditation. Pause for a few seconds at each ellipsis (. . .).

- Standing up for your values and the rights of others is not always easy. We have a need to belong, and we don't like to be rejected. No one does. Jesus knows that. He was always standing up for others.

  The people he helped were sometimes embarrassed but always appreciative. Jesus had to stand by his values, and he invites us to do the same.

  Imagine yourself on a desert road back in the time of Jesus. . . . The air is hot and dry. . . . There's a slight wind every once in a while that kicks up the dirt and sand. . . . Behind you is the village you just left, and in front of you are fields worked by farmers. . . . This is their means of survival, their livelihood. . . . As the sun covers the field of wheat, the stalks appear golden. . . . You stop to admire the beautiful scene. . . . There is no one working today because it is the Sabbath. . . . It is the Lord's day. . . . The Law states that no one is to work on the Sabbath. . . .

  In the distance you see a small group of people gathered, looking at the field. . . . As you get closer, you hear them arguing about something. . . . You recognize some of the people. . . . The farmer and his wife who own the field look distressed. . . . Two of the local Pharisees—the town officials—are there arguing with the farmer and his wife. . . .

  You now see Jesus and two of his Apostles approach the group. . . . The farmer and his wife look relieved to see Jesus. . . . As you get closer, you see and hear the cause of the discussion. . . . Stuck in a ditch in the field is the farmer's ox. . . . You hear the animal cry in pain. . . . Why isn't anyone doing anything you wonder? . . .

  Now you are next to the crowd and can hear the conversation. . . . The farmer wants to help the ox out of the ditch. . . . The Pharisees claim that doing so would be work, and no one is permitted to work on the Sabbath. . . . That takes you by surprise. . . . Surely helping an injured animal could not be considered work. . . . It is mercy. . . .

  Now everyone turns to Jesus for his opinion. . . . Jesus says it is not against God's Law to help a suffering animal. . . . The Pharisees storm away in anger. . . . The farmer and his wife are relieved. . . .

  Jesus invites you to walk with him and discuss what just happened. . . . Jesus asks you: "What do you think I should have done—what I did, walk away, or wait until the Pharisees left and helped the farmer in private?" Spend a few minutes talking with Jesus. [Longer pause.]

Tell Jesus about a time when you were a victim of prejudice. Describe what helped you through it. [Longer pause.]

Tell Jesus about a time when you helped someone else who was being victimized. [Longer pause.]

If you could change one situation in your life, which one would you change and why? [Longer pause.]

Would you like to talk to Jesus about anything else before he goes? [Longer pause.]

Jesus says: "I know what it's like to be rejected. . . . But that doesn't mean rejection defeated me. . . . In many ways it made me a stronger person. . . . When I felt really down, what got me through was prayer. . . . God is always with me, strengthening me, and I am with you. . . . Always believe in yourself and your values."

Before he leaves, Jesus wants to give you a sign of friendship to strengthen you. . . . Feel Jesus make the sign of the cross on your forehead as he says, "This is for the gift of wisdom." . . . Feel him make the sign of the cross on your eyes as he says, "This is for the gift to see each person as I do." . . . Feel him make the sign of the cross on your mouth as he says, "This is for the gift to speak the truth." . . . Feel him make the sign of the cross on your hands and say, "This is for the gift to build a world of harmony and peace." . . .

Jesus leaves now. . . . He walks back down the road toward the village. . . . Now you sit down on the side of the road, close your eyes, and say a little prayer of thanks: "Jesus, thank you for showing me the way to live through rejection without being defeated. It still hurts at times, so please continue to guide me. When I do stand up for myself or another, I truly feel courageous and heroic. Guide me in all things. Thank you for being my special friend and guide."

When you open your eyes, you will no longer be sitting on the road but back here in this room. When you are ready, slowly open your eyes and come back.

Evaluation

Large Group (5 minutes)

After the guided meditation, direct the teens to reflect in writing on the following questions. Invite them to answer aloud if they feel comfortable doing so.

- If you had only one word to describe today, what word would you pick?
- What is one new thing you learned today, or what is one thing you really liked? (It could be something we did or something someone said.)
- What do you feel God is challenging you to do as a result of this retreat?

Culture Cake

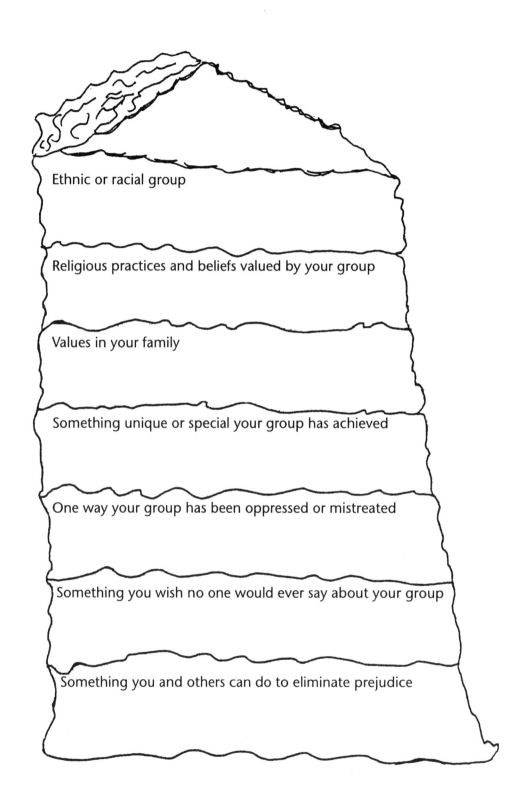

Ethnic or racial group

Religious practices and beliefs valued by your group

Values in your family

Something unique or special your group has achieved

One way your group has been oppressed or mistreated

Something you wish no one would ever say about your group

Something you and others can do to eliminate prejudice

Handout 1–A: Permission to reproduce this handout for use in your program is granted.

Retreat 2

Graduation

Theme This retreat helps graduates bring closure to their high school years, discuss their hopes and fears, and realize that God continues to walk with them on their life journey.

Bible Basis *Josh. 1:9.* Just as Joshua trusted in God, so, too, can the teens appreciate God's constant love for them.

Objectives The retreatants will do the following:
- identify areas of personal growth during their high school years
- reflect on the Scriptures and see them as a source of strength during a transitional time
- name specific fears and hopes for their future, and see these as opportunities for growth
- identify and name their goals for the future
- affirm one another's gifts and talents

Retreat at a Glance

The following chart offers a brief overview of the retreat activities, time frames, and materials needed. For more detailed information about any of the activities, refer to the directions given in the Retreat in Detail section.

Note: The handouts for this retreat need to be made into a booklet before the retreat.

ACTIVITY	TIME FRAME	SUPPLIES
Welcome and Introduction	10–15 minutes	poster with standards
Icebreakers	15–30 minutes	depends on selection
Opening Prayer	5 minutes	Bible
My Yearbook	15–20 minutes	handout booklets, pencils
Farewell Gift	20–30 minutes	paper cups
Memory Charades	15 minutes	
Break	10 minutes	
Growing Up	20–25 minutes	booklets, pencils, Bible
Past and Future	20–30 minutes	booklets, pencils, newsprint, markers
Lunch	45 minutes	
Icebreakers	15 minutes	depends on selection
Future Aspirations	20 minutes	marker, paper, tape, booklets, pencils
God's Love Is Everlasting	15 minutes	booklets, pencils
Ten-Year Reunion	20 minutes	booklets, pencils
Farewell Flattery	20–30 minutes	booklets, pencils, background music, tape or CD player
Closing Guided Meditation	20–30 minutes	instrumental music, tape or CD player
Evaluation	5 minutes	pencils, paper

Retreat in Detail

Welcome and Introduction (10–15 minutes)

Icebreakers (15–30 minutes)
Choose from among the icebreakers offered in part A of the appendix of this book, or use games of your own.

Opening Prayer (5 minutes)
Begin the prayer by reading Josh. 1:9, which is an account of Joshua's trust in God.

Finish with the following prayer, or a similar one:

- Dear God, you promised Joshua that you would be with him as he led your people into unknown lands. Help us to remember that you are with us, too, as we venture into new experiences after graduation. As we plan for the future, free us from the anxiety that moving to a new place in our life can bring, and reassure us of your unending love. Amen.

My Yearbook Small-Group Activity (15–20 minutes)
In this activity the teens reflect on the highlights of their high school years.

Ask the retreatants to form small groups, and give each person a handout booklet and a pencil. Let them scan through the whole booklet if they choose. Many will want to anyway.

Direct the teens to open their booklet to page 1, and introduce the activity "My Yearbook" this way:

- It's yearbook time, and you get to write whatever you want about yourself! Take a few minutes to complete the page. You will have an opportunity to share, if you wish, with other group members.

Give the young people time to complete the page. When they are done, explain the following instructions to the whole group:

- Now you will have a chance to share what you wrote with the other members of your small group. Each small group needs a leader. The job of the leader is to go first and share his or her answer to the sentence completion in the first box, "I was voted most likely to . . ." Then the leader ensures that everyone in the group gets a chance to complete that statement. Continue in this fashion until each of the sentence starters has been discussed. It's important to share not only what you wrote but why you wrote it. Let's have the oldest person in each group be the leader for this exercise. Any questions?

Give the groups time to discuss the sentence starters. When they are finished, lead a discussion based on the following questions (see the introduction for alternative ways of debriefing this and other retreat activities):

- Why are yearbooks important?
- How did you feel as you recalled your high school memories?
- What was some of the parting advice you had for your classmates?

Farewell Gift

Small-Group Activity (20–30 minutes)

In this activity the teens acknowledge the relationships they have formed during high school and express their gratitude for these relationships with a gift.

Give each teen a paper cup. Instruct them with words similar to the following:

- You have just recalled some fond memories and experiences you have shared with your classmates, and you want to leave them with a special gift. However, all you can find is this paper cup. Take this cup and use it to create a symbol of something you would like to give the graduating class of your school. You can make your symbol by tearing or folding the cup any way you want, and by adding items from this room. For example, one young person once made the cup into a phone to represent keeping in touch. He punched a hole in the bottom of the cup and attached a string. Another student tore the cup into a heart shape to represent the gift of love she wanted to give her classmates. Please complete the exercise in silence. You will have time to share your symbol with your small-group members.

Allow enough time for the teens to complete their gift. Then continue with this set of instructions.

- Each of you will now have the opportunity to share with your small group the gift you have created and explain why you want to give it to your graduating class. The person with the shortest first name will begin.

When the small groups are finished sharing their gifts, tell them to combine their gifts into one gift or a collection of gifts. Then direct each small group to present its gift or gifts to the whole group with a brief explanation.

Conclude the activity by having the small groups applaud one another. Leave the gifts on display for the remainder of the retreat.

Memory Charades

Small-Group Activity (15 minutes)

The purpose of this activity is for the teens to recall one significant event from their high school years.

Have each small group design a charade (with no speaking) of a school memory that most people in the other groups would likely be able to identify. Caution the teens not to use situations that may embarrass their peers or teachers. Allow 5 minutes of preparation. Then invite the small groups to perform their charade with the nonperforming groups guessing the memory it represents.

Conclude the activity in your own words:

- God has blessed us with memories. They keep us in touch with our experiences, our growth, and the people who have touched our life.

Break

(10 minutes)

Growing Up

Small-Group Activity (20–25 minutes)

This activity helps the teens understand that all growth entails change.

1. Have the retreatants turn to page 2 in their booklet, "Growing Up." Introduce the activity this way:

- We go through many changes as we grow up. Change is a part of life. Let's take a look at some of the changes you have gone through and survived.

  Instruct everyone to complete the chart for themselves. Ask them to try to recall what they looked like at the various stages of life listed, then to remember what they wore at each age, and so on.

2. After everyone is done filling out the chart, give these directions:
- Now you will have an opportunity to share with the members of your small group some of the ways you have grown and changed. First you are to choose one category and talk about the change you went through. After everyone has shared once, continue sharing your responses to as many categories as possible until time is called. The leader goes first in each case and makes sure everyone has a chance to share. Let's have the leader be the youngest person in each group. Any questions?

3. After the groups have completed their discussion, call for a volunteer to read Josh. 1:9. If the group is unfamiliar with who Joshua is, give a brief description in your own words:
- The Book of Joshua could be a great script for an action-packed movie. It's filled with spies, surprise attacks, guerrilla warfare, courageous leaders, unusual battles, and victory celebrations.

  The central hero is Joshua, a creative military mind with great organizational skills. But above all, he is absolutely loyal to and dependent on God.

  The plot tells how the Israelites conquered land God promised to their ancestor Abram. . . . Their parents had escaped from Egypt but had not followed God. So the whole generation that left Egypt had died in the desert, leaving the children—under Joshua's leadership—to cross the Jordan River and conquer the land of Canaan.

  Canaan consisted of many independent cities, each with its own king and army, and many had strong, high walls. So the Israelites had to defeat the cities one by one, beginning with the famous battle of Jericho.

  Two major themes flow through Joshua. First, the book shows how God works through people to fulfill [God's] purposes on earth. And it emphasizes the importance of loyally following God, depending on God's power in all things. (Adapted from Youth Bible, pp. 194–195)

4. Discuss the following questions with the whole group:
- Are changes good or bad? Why?
- Are changes difficult or easy?
- Why are we afraid of change?
- What changes did some students mention that you had never thought of before?
- Would you say that you are happy with most of the changes in your life? Why or why not?
- How do you feel about the major changes that you will be facing after high school?
- Would you like to go back and live your high school years over again? Why or why not?

5. Offer a conclusion to the activity in your own words:

- Even though we go through so many changes during our life, we can trust one constant: God is the same yesterday, today, and tomorrow. Some changes we look forward to—like getting our driver's license. Other changes may be a little scary—like breaking up with a boyfriend or girlfriend, or going away to school. The fact is we are always changing, sometimes in ways we don't even notice. And as we go through this retreat, we hope to see that through all these changes, God has been with us and will continue to be with us.

Past and Future

Small-Group Activity (20–30 minutes)

In this activity the teens reflect on their fears of graduating, their hopes for the future, and their accomplishments during high school.

Have the teens turn to page 3 in their booklet, "Past and Future," and complete the handout individually. When they are finished, give each small group a piece of newsprint and a marker and the following instructions:

- For this exercise you need a group recorder and a reporter. The recorder writes down the things that the group members share. The reporter reads aloud to the whole group what is on the small group's newsprint. The recorder goes first and shares her or his fears about graduating. Then everyone in the small group shares their fears, and the recorder writes them down on the newsprint. Next, in the same fashion, the leader and the other group members share their hopes for the future. When you get to achievements, everyone shares their most significant achievement and what they had to go through to achieve it. Continue until everyone has shared. Let's have the recorder be the person in each group with the shortest hair, and the reporter be the person with the longest hair. Any questions?

After the small groups are finished, direct the reporters to share their group's newsprint list with the whole group.

Conclude by asking the whole group these questions:
- What does this exercise say about growing up?
- What are the purposes of fears and hopes in our life?
- What would it be like to live in a world without fears or hopes?

Lunch

(45 minutes)

Icebreakers

(15 minutes)
Choose from among the icebreakers offered in part A of the appendix of this book, or use games of your own.

Future Aspirations

Large-Group Activity (20 minutes)

In this activity the retreatants prioritize their future goals.

Before the activity, write each of the numbers 1 to 12 on a separate sheet of paper. Mark off a section of the floor in twelve equal lengths and tape the sheets of paper in numerical order to the floor.

Direct the teens to open their booklet to page 6, "Future Aspirations," and give them the following directions:

- Listed on page 6 are twelve possible goals for your future. Your job is to rank them in order of importance, with 1 being your most important goal, 2 your next important goal, and so on. If some of the goals listed don't reflect your aspirations at all, leave them blank. Then write your own aspirations in the spaces provided and include these in your ranking instead.

When the teens have completed their ranking, offer these instructions:

- I'm going to read aloud the aspirations for your future. After I read each one, you are to stand near the number that you wrote down for that aspiration, which indicates its priority to you. If you did not rank a particular item, just stand off to the side. After you take a stand, I'm going to ask volunteers to explain their ranking.

If you have time, read all twelve goals. If not, select as many as time will allow, or ask the teens which goals they would like to discuss. After the teens have moved to the spot that matches their ranking, invite volunteers to explain their choice.

Conclude the activity by leading a whole-group discussion of these questions:

- What aspirations do you have that were not on this list?
- What do your aspirations say about your values?
- How do you decide which is more important—your aspirations or your values?

God's Love Is Everlasting

Small-Group Activity (15 minutes)
In this activity the teens see the Scriptures as a source of support to guide them through life's ups and downs.

1. Introduce the activity by conveying this information in your own words:

- God has been with us during the changes in our life so far. So we can trust that God will continue to be with us during future events. We can gain encouragement from the stories of Abraham, Moses, Joshua, and Mary. Many passages in the Scriptures reveal God's constant love for us, reassuring us that we are never alone. Open your booklet to page 7, "God's Love Is Everlasting." Each small group will be assigned one of the Scripture passages listed there. After reading your assigned Scripture passage, please discuss these three questions:
  - When have you known this to be true?
  - Why is it hard to believe this?
  - What would help you believe this more completely?

  In order for the teens to understand how to do this exercise, share a personal experience from your life that answers those questions.

2. Assign each small group a Scripture passage from page 7 and give the following directions:

- Each group needs a reader to read the Scripture passage, a recorder to write down your group's answers, and a reporter to share aloud what your small group discusses. You may pick your own representatives, or you can have the reader be the person whose birthday is closest to Christmas; the recorder, the person whose birthday is closest to Saint Patrick's Day; and the reporter, the person whose birthday is closest to Halloween. Any questions?

After all the small groups are finished, have the reporters share their group's answers with the whole group.

Ten-Year Reunion

Small-Group Activity (20 minutes)

In this activity the teens encourage one another to pursue their goals by imagining one another's future.

1. Form the teens into groups of no more than four or five, and have them open their booklet to page 8, "Ten-Year Reunion." Give the following directions:
- Imagine that you are ten years older than you are right now, and you are walking into your ten-year high school reunion. When you get inside, you sit at a table with the other people in your small group. You begin to discuss what life has been like for the past ten years. In your booklet, complete a chart for each person in your small group, indicating how you see each of them ten years from now.

Note: If the teens in your group do not attend the same high school and do not know one another well, you may want to adapt the activity by having them each foretell their own future.

Give the teens time to complete the form. Then call time and explain these instructions:
- The person with the longest last name will be the first to have his or her future foretold by the other group members. The person who is being talked about should remain silent until everyone has shared what they wrote. Then he or she may comment. Continue until everyone in your small group has had their future foretold. Any questions?

2. When all the groups are finished, lead a discussion with the whole group based on the following questions:
- Did you like this activity? Why or why not?
- How many of you are excited about your future? Explain.
- Did anyone say anything about your future that you hope comes true? Explain.
- Would you feel comfortable having someone else choose your future for you? Explain.

3. Conclude the activity in the following way:
- We all have hopes for our future. What others see us doing may not be what we think we will be doing. The future can be interesting, exciting, and also a little scary for us. And though no one really knows exactly what it holds, we do know that God is interested in our future and is with us wherever we go.

Farewell Flattery

Affirmation (20–30 minutes)

In this activity the teens affirm one another for the gifts they appreciate about one another as seen during their high school years together.

Direct the teens to open their booklet to the center pages (pages 4 and 5), which are blank. Have them put their first and last name in large letters in the center of the two-page spread. Then instruct them by saying something like this:

- Beginning first in your own small group, exchange booklets and write something in each person's booklet—something you learned from that person, something you admire about her or him, or something for which you want to thank her or him.

  After you have finished writing to each person in your group, you may travel to the other small groups. You may not get to everyone, and that's okay. Please don't write things like, "Let's get together soon." Rather, write an affirmation—something you appreciate about each person.

  In the background play an appropriate song, such as Michael W. Smith's "Friends." Give the young people time to write in one another's booklets. When time is up, have them return to their small groups and read to themselves what others wrote. Next, give directions like these:
- Pick a couple of the things people wrote about you that you really like. If you want to, share those with the other people in your small group.

  Be alert to the possibility that some teens may be new to the school or to your youth group and may not have a lot of friends. Make sure other teens or adult advisers write something in their booklets so that they don't feel left out.

Closing Guided Meditation

(20–30 minutes)

Begin the meditation with a progressive muscle relaxation exercise (see part C of the appendix for suggestions). If possible, play soft instrumental background music. Then continue with the following guided meditation. Pause for a few seconds at each ellipsis (. . .).

- As we go through life, we make new friends and grow apart from others. We succeed, and we also falter. The book of our life has many chapters, and new chapters usually begin when something significant happens—like graduation. Through it all, we need to remember that God is always with us.

  Imagine yourself back in the time of Jesus, standing on the shore of a lake. . . . You are standing with some of the disciples. . . . Most of them fish for a living, so they are dressed in rough clothing. . . . In the water is a rather large rowboat. . . . Jesus has invited the group to go to the other side of the lake and pray with him for a little while. . . . It is late afternoon, and the sun is slowly turning an orange and red shade as it begins to set. . . . The weather is pleasant, and the water is calm. . . . Since everyone has fished frequently, traveling on the water at dusk is not a problem. . . .

  All of you get into the boat and begin to row. . . . No one is in a hurry. . . . Everyone seems to be enjoying this peaceful time with Jesus. . . . The disciples usually work six full days a week because fishing is their only source of income. . . . So to relax with Jesus is truly a treat. . . .

  Jesus settles into the back of the boat. . . . He looks very tired. . . . As you get to the middle of the lake, the wind suddenly picks up—from out of nowhere. . . . Everyone is struggling with the oars to keep the boat afloat. . . . Waves are spewing water into the boat, and some disciples are using their hands to scoop the water out. . . .

You notice that Jesus has been asleep this whole time. . . . Asleep! . . . The disciples' lives are at stake, and he is sleeping! . . . You are outraged! . . . Finally Peter goes over and wakes Jesus, saying, "Lord, save us! We will drown!" . . .

Jesus answers: "Why are you afraid? You don't have enough faith." . . . Jesus gets up and raises his hands, and the wind and the waves completely calm down. . . . You look around and see the amazed looks on everyone's faces. . . . You, too, are amazed and realize you have just witnessed a miracle. . . .

Jesus now invites you to sit down next to him in the boat and tell him about some of the rough, stormy times in your life. . . . Maybe for you, graduation is one of them. . . . Spend some time talking with Jesus. [Longer pause.]

Jesus says: "Maybe during some of your tough times you didn't think I was with you; perhaps you thought that I was asleep. . . . But I knew. . . . It just took you some time to realize that the storm had to take its course before calming down, but I was always with you. . . . Some tough times take a long time to heal, so I have given you people on earth to help you. . . . Tell me about some people who have supported you." [Longer pause.]

Now Jesus asks: "What are some of your qualities and talents that you bring into the world as you graduate? [Longer pause.]

"What are some things about graduating that you look forward to? [Longer pause.]

"What are some of your fears and concerns? [Longer pause.]

"What are some of your goals in life, and how can I help you achieve them?" [Longer pause.]

The boat has almost reached the other shore now. . . . Jesus asks if there's anything else you want to talk about before everyone gets out of the boat. . . . Spend these last few moments talking with Jesus or just listening to him. [Longer pause.]

The boat now lands, and everyone but you and Jesus gets out of the boat. . . . As Jesus leaves the boat, he rests his hand on your shoulder, looks into your eyes, and says, "I am always with you.". . .

You don't want to get out of the boat just yet because it is so peaceful here. . . . So you close your eyes and pray: "Dear Lord, thank you for being with me during the storms of my life and the joys, too. I love this feeling of peace, and I ask for this gift to remain with me. Let me never forget that you love me and are always there to guide, support, and help—if only I ask. Bless my classmates and those who have supported me. Let me share the good news of your love and peace wherever I go."

When you open your eyes, you will no longer be in the boat but back here in this room. When you are ready, slowly open your eyes and come back.

Invite any faculty members or other adults who are present to come to the front, extend their right hands, and recite the "Blessing Over the Graduates," found on page 9 of the booklet.

Evaluation   Large Group (5 minutes)

After the guided meditation, direct the teens to reflect in writing on the following questions. Invite them to answer aloud if they feel comfortable doing so.

- If you had only one word to describe today, what word would you pick?
- What is one new thing you learned today, or what is one thing you really liked? (It could be something we did or something someone said.)
- What do you feel God is challenging you to do as a result of this retreat?

Handout Booklet

(The handouts for this retreat get made into a handout booklet. This is accomplished by photocopying the handouts so that they are double-sided and stapling them together. All the handouts except handout 2–E are provided here; handout 2–E is two blank pages you provide yourself. Directions for each handout follow below.

Handout 2–A. "We Are God's Work of Art," is provided here for you to reproduce. It is the front cover of the booklet.

Handout 2–B. "My Yearbook" is provided here for you to reproduce. This handout is page 1.

Handout 2–C. "Growing Up" is provided here for you to reproduce. This handout is page 2.

Handout 2–D. "Past and Future" is provided here for you to reproduce. This handout is page 3.

Handout 2–E. You provide it. It is two blank sheets of paper numbered as pages 4 and 5. These pages are used for written affirmations in the Farewell Flattery activity. (If you leave the reverse sides of pages 3 and 6 blank, you will have the pages you need for this activity.)

Handout 2–F. "Future Aspirations" is provided here for you to reproduce. This handout is page 6.

Handout 2–G. "God's Love Is Everlasting" is provided here for you to reproduce. This handout is page 7.

Handout 2–H. "Ten-Year Reunion" is provided here for you to reproduce. This handout is page 8.

Handout 2–I. "Blessing Over the Graduates" is provided here for you to reproduce. This handout is page 9. Add a blank page following page 9 to serve as the back cover of the booklet.

We are God's work of Art

created in
Christ Jesus
for the good works
that will make up
our way of life.

My Yearbook

Draw or write your answers to each of the following:

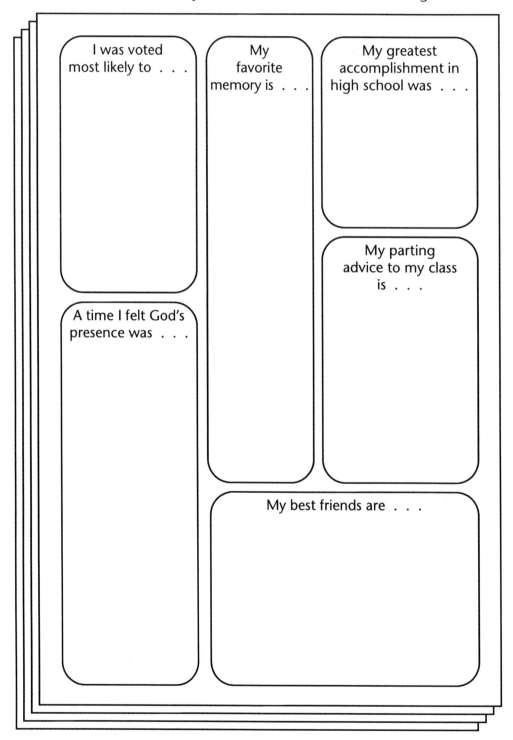

I was voted
most likely to . . .

My
favorite
memory is . . .

My greatest
accomplishment in
high school was . . .

My parting
advice to my class
is . . .

A time I felt God's
presence was . . .

My best friends are . . .

1

Growing Up

	Age 0–5	Age 5–10	Now	10 years from now
I wore				
I was best friends with				
I was afraid to				
I thought of God as				
My favorite TV show was				
I didn't know				
Games I played				
I was not allowed to				
I loved				
I was good at				
I never				

My most significant or meaningful change was . . . because . . .

2

Past and Future

Fears I have about graduating . . .

Hopes I have for my future . . .

 What I have achieved or how I have grown
during my past four years of high school . . .

3

Future Aspirations

_____ to be successful in my career

_____ to have a strong marriage and family life

_____ to have lots of money

_____ to have plenty of free time for recreation and hobbies

_____ to travel around the world

_____ to have strong friendships

_____ to make a contribution to my community or society

_____ to be able to give my children better opportunities than I've had

_____ to live close to my parents and relatives

_____ to move away from this area of the country

_____ to work to correct social and economic inequalities

_____ to find purpose and meaning in my life

_____ [an aspiration I have:] _____

_____ [an aspiration I have:] _____

_____ [an aspiration I have:] _____

6

Handout 2–F: Permission to reproduce this handout for use in your program is granted.

47

God's Love Is Everlasting

"Remember that I commanded you to be strong and brave. Don't be afraid, because God will be with you everywhere you go." (Adapted from Joshua 1:9)

You give me new strength. You lead me on paths that are right for the good of your name. Even if I walk through a very dark valley, I will not be afraid, because you are with me. (Adapted from Psalm 23:3–4)

God is our protection and our strength, an ever-present help in times of trouble. (Adapted from Psalm 46:1)

God, you are my hope. God, I have trusted you since I was young. I have depended on you since I was born; you helped me even on the day of my birth. (Adapted from Psalm 71:5–6)

Trust in God with all your heart, and don't depend on your own understanding. Remember God in all you do, and God will give you success. (Adapted from Proverbs 3:5–6)

Depend on God in whatever you do, and your plans will succeed. God makes everything go as God pleases. (Adapted from Proverbs 16:3–4)

"I leave you peace; my peace I give you. I do not give it to you as the world does. So don't let your heart be troubled or afraid." (Adapted from John 14:27)

Praise be to the God and Father of our Lord Jesus Christ. God is the Father who is full of mercy and all comfort. God comforts us every time we have trouble, so when others have trouble, we can comfort them with the same comfort God gives us. (Adapted from 2 Corinthians 1:3–4)

1. When have you known this to be true?
2. Why is it hard to believe this?
3. What would help you believe this more completely?

7

Ten-Year Reunion

Name	
Career or current job	
Family status	
Car you are driving	
Where you live	
Place you have visited	
Greatest achievement since high school	
Goals for the next ten years	
Other	

Name	
Career or current job	
Family status	
Car you are driving	
Where you live	
Place you have visited	
Greatest achievement since high school	
Goals for the next ten years	
Other	

Name	
Career or current job	
Family status	
Car you are driving	
Where you live	
Place you have visited	
Greatest achievement since high school	
Goals for the next ten years	
Other	

Name	
Career or current job	
Family status	
Car you are driving	
Where you live	
Place you have visited	
Greatest achievement since high school	
Goals for the next ten years	
Other	

8

Handout 2–H: Permission to reproduce this handout for use in your program is granted.

49

Blessing Over the Graduates

Spirit of Wisdom, whose truth fills our world
and invites us into a lifetime of learning,
bless these graduates.
Give them joy and a sense of accomplishment in
what they have achieved.
But give them also a thirst for knowledge.
Make them seekers who will enjoy the process of discovery.
Let their education go beyond classrooms and books.
Sensitize them to the lessons of experience and
the wisdom of the heart.
Open them to faith as well as reason,
intuition as well as logic.
Give them a curiosity that goes beyond
partial answers and old insights.
But through all their life give them an inner peace
so they are neither inflated by what they know
nor frustrated by what is still beyond their grasp.
Abiding teacher, may this graduation that they will celebrate
signal the beginning of their larger education.
Bless them and all of us with your wisdom and peace.
Amen.

(Jim Dinn, *The Fire of Peace: A Prayer Book,* compiled and edited
by Mary Lou Kownacki, OSB [Erie, PA: Pax Christi USA, 1992], pages 64–65)

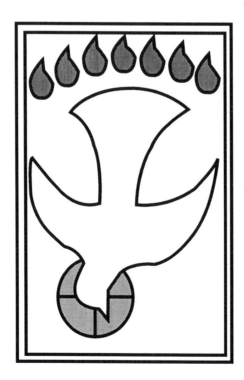

9

Retreat 3

Peacemaking

Theme   This retreat explores the causes of injustice, and it helps the retreatants discover ways to be peacemakers.

Bible Basis   *Luke 16:19–31.* In the story of Lazarus and the rich man, Jesus reminds us to have compassion for others and, through justice, to bring peace to the lives of others.

Objectives   The retreatants will do the following:
- assess attitudes concerning issues of justice and peace
- recall a biblical as well as a historical mandate for a Christian response to suffering, inequity, and injustice
- reflect on the unjust structures of society that keep power in the hands of a few
- recognize the problems of unjust social situations
- be challenged to follow in Christ's footsteps by working for justice

Retreat at a Glance

The following chart offers a brief overview of the retreat activities, time frames, and materials needed. For more detailed information about any of the activities, refer to the directions given in the Retreat in Detail section.

ACTIVITY	TIME FRAME	SUPPLIES
Welcome and Introduction	10–15 minutes	poster with standards
Icebreakers	15–30 minutes	depends on selection
Opening Prayer	5 minutes	Bible
Peace	10 minutes	newsprint, marker
Peacemaking *Jeopardy*	20–25 minutes	*Jeopardy* game board, construction paper, markers, masking tape
Cooperative Thumb Wrestling	10 minutes	Bibles
Break	10 minutes	
Anytown U.S.A.	60–75 minutes	see the materials needed list in the activity
Lunch	45 minutes	
Icebreakers	15 minutes	depends on selection
Lazarus Skit	15–30 minutes	resource 3–C, props
Charitable	15–20 minutes	Bibles
Works of Mercy	20 minutes	banner with works of mercy, blank paper, markers, masking tape
Classified Ad	15–20 minutes	paper, pencils
Peace Revisited	10 minutes	definition of peace (brainstormed earlier), newsprint, markers
Closing Guided Meditation	20–30 minutes	instrumental music, tape or CD player
Evaluation	5 minutes	pencils, paper

Retreat in Detail

Welcome and Introduction (10–15 minutes)

Icebreakers (15–30 minutes)
Choose from among the icebreakers offered in part A of the appendix of this book, or use games of your own.

Opening Prayer (5 minutes)
Begin the prayer by reading aloud the story of Lazarus and the rich man from Luke 16:19–31. Finish with a prayer similar to this one:
- Dear God, the story of Lazarus and the rich man reminds us to be grateful for the many blessings we have, and to reach out to help those who are less fortunate than ourselves. The story also reminds us that we are not all born with similar opportunities. Therefore, those with fewer opportunities have a responsibility to help those with less opportunities. It is not always easy to sacrifice for others. Help me, God, to thank you for the gifts and opportunities you have bestowed on me. Give me the courage to stand with people who need my help and support, so that all of us may share in the wealth of your Reign. Amen.

Peace Large-Group Brainstorming (10 minutes)
In this activity the retreatants brainstorm definitions of the word *peace*.

On a sheet of newsprint, write the word *peace* in large letters. Invite the retreatants to call out words and images that come to mind when they hear this term.

Leave the brainstormed responses posted, because at the end of the retreat the group will repeat the brainstorming and see if any of their attitudes toward peacemaking have changed.

Conclude the activity by asking this question:
- During this retreat we are going to explore our attitudes toward peace. Do you believe that peace is possible? If so, why? If not, why not?

✓ Peacemaking *Jeopardy* Small-Group Activity (20–25 minutes)
This game serves as an introductory activity on peace. Its objective is to show that examples from the Scriptures and from our history illustrate that peace is an important Christian value.

Before the retreat, create a *Jeopardy* game board. On a large piece of poster board, make three columns, one labeled "Saints," a second, "Scriptures," and a third, "Historical Events." The statements and questions for the game, along with the point values for correct questions, are given on the next two pages. (In *Jeopardy* the answers are called questions because they are phrased in the form of a question.) Write the statements beneath their respective columns, as listed below. Do not write the questions in brackets on the poster. Cut out fifteen rectangular pieces of construction paper. Write a point value on each rectangle as follows: three cards labeled 100, three cards labeled 200, three cards labeled 300, three cards labeled 400, and three cards labeled 500. Use masking tape or any other easily removable adhesive to place the construction-paper rectangles over the statements, matching the point numbers with the point value assigned to each statement. Here are the categories, statements, and questions:

Saints

100 points
- She won the 1979 Nobel Peace Prize for her work with "the poorest of the poor" in India, where her religious order cares for sick and dying people, and poor and outcast people. [Who is Mother Teresa of Calcutta?]

200 points
- As a young man living in thirteenth-century Italy, he gave up his inheritance to devote himself to God's work of caring for sick people and poor people. The religious order he founded is now one of the largest in the world. [Who is Francis of Assisi?]

300 points
- She faced oppression from family and friends because of her decision to convert to Roman Catholicism. Eventually she founded the Sisters of Charity in the United States and laid the foundation for the U.S. parochial school system. [Who is Elizabeth Ann Seton?]

400 points
- As the archbishop of San Salvador, in El Salvador, he spoke out fearlessly against injustice and the oppression of poor people. In 1980, while celebrating Mass, he was murdered for expressing his antigovernment views openly. [Who is Oscar Romero?]

500 points
- In seventeenth-century France, these two people cared for sick people they found on the streets. They were cofounders of the Sisters of Charity. Their work marked the beginning of Catholic hospitals. [Who are Vincent de Paul and Louise de Marillac?]

Scriptures

100 points
- In this parable Jesus shocked his listeners, because the hero in the story turns out to be from a group that was disrespected by the Jews of Jerusalem. One of Jesus' messages in this parable is not to judge people on the basis of their religious practice, but rather by the good works they do. [What is the parable of the good Samaritan?]

200 points
- This is the central story in the Hebrew Scriptures. It is a powerful story of liberation, teaching us that God desires us to be free. [What is the Exodus?]

300 points
- These unpopular messengers in the Hebrew Scriptures books issued a challenge to the people of their day—a call for moral transformation. [Who are the prophets?]

400 points
- This is the central message of Jesus' teaching. For Jesus this would become reality when unconditional love rules in the hearts of all people. [What is the Reign (or Kingdom) of God?]

500 points
- Reluctantly he responded to God's call to preach to the Ninevites. He was surprised when they repented and God saved them. [Who is Jonah?]

Historical Events

100 points
- The signing of this document was considered an illegal act of treason because it declared the colonies to be free of British rule. [What is the Declaration of Independence?]

200 points
- The colonists waged a campaign of direct action in response to an unjust tax levied upon them to help pay British war debts. Private property was destroyed in Boston. [What is the Boston Tea Party?]

300 points
- This movement in the late 1800s was an effort to change the law that prohibited women from voting. [Answer: What is the Women's Suffrage movement?]

400 points
- The goal of this movement was to put an end to legal discrimination in the United States. It hoped to ensure equal protection under the law for all United States' citizens. Boycotts, marches, and rallies were some strategies used to gain attention for the cause. [What is the Civil Rights movement?]

500 points
- This was a secret network of "safe houses" set up to harbor runaway slaves as they illegally made their way to the North. [What is the Underground Railroad?]

    The following bonus questions are optional. They can be read aloud and assigned a value of 1000 points.
- He was a Roman Catholic priest who voluntarily took the place of a prisoner who was condemned to die by starvation in a German concentration camp during World War II. He was canonized in 1982. [Who is Maximilian Kolbe?]
- In 1955 she refused to move to the rear of the bus, as was required of blacks in the South. Her arrest led to a 381-day bus boycott in Montgomery, Alabama. [Who is Rosa Parks?]
- Defying the male-dominated medical profession, she became the first woman doctor in the United States in 1849. [Who is Elizabeth Blackwell?]
- He was a first-century convert from Judaism to Christianity who was arrested for preaching the Gospel and eventually killed for his belief in Jesus Christ. [Who is Saint Paul?]
- This bishop won the Nobel Peace Prize in 1985 for his leadership in the South African civil rights struggle. [Who is Desmond Tutu?]

1. The game is played like the TV game show *Jeopardy.* Begin by dividing the retreatants into three small groups. Randomly name them Team A, Team B, and Team C. Post the *Jeopardy* game board. Give the whole group the following instructions:

- We are now going to play Peacemaking *Jeopardy.* You must elect a spokesperson for your team. This is the only person who can give your team's response. Your team will have a chance to discuss your response before the spokesperson shares it. If someone other than the spokesperson answers, your response will be disqualified, and another team will have a chance to answer. All responses must be stated in the form of a question. The teams will take turns choosing a category and a point value. We will start by having Team A choose a category and a point value. It must then attempt to respond to the corresponding statement correctly. If Team A answers correctly, it scores the designated number of points. If it answers incorrectly, it does not lose points, but Team B gets a chance to respond to the same statement. This continues until a correct response has been given or every team has tried to answer and cannot. At the end of the game, the team with the most points wins.

2. Play the game and declare a winner. Then lead a discussion with the whole group based on the following questions (see the introduction for alternative ways of debriefing this and other retreat activities):

- Why are these categories—saints, Scriptures, and historical events—appropriate for a retreat on peacemaking?
- What do the categories have in common?
- What are some other examples from the Scriptures in which people challenged the laws and policies of the time?

   If the teens have trouble coming up with answers to the last question, you can provide the following examples:

- One example of an act of nonviolent civil disobedience was the refusal of the Hebrew midwives to kill the male offspring of Hebrew mothers.
- Jesus destroyed private property in the Temple. (Jesus was later arrested, tried for treason, and executed as a subversive.)
- Jesus was resurrected from the dead. (The Roman state had Jesus put to death, and the burial vault was closed with the Roman seal. When the state puts you to death, you are supposed to stay dead. With the breaking of that seal, God became an accomplice in the greatest escape of all time.)
- Peter and Paul's teaching declaring that "Jesus Christ is Lord" was considered a capital offense of treason. They were imprisoned and executed by the state.

3. Continue by posing this question:

- What are some examples from the history of the United States in which people challenged the unjust laws and policies of the day?
   You may need to provide examples like the following:

- Some people helped slaves escape from slavery through the Underground Railroad.
- Many U.S. citizens protested U.S. involvement in the war in Vietnam.

Explain that in each case, campaigns of direct action—some involving civil disobedience—challenged the values and laws of the land by appealing to a higher sense of justice. Types of direct action include strikes, boycotts, demonstrations, prayer vigils, and so on.

4. Conclude the activity by conveying the following information in your own words:

- As followers of Jesus, we are called upon to imitate him not only in our own life but also in our relationships with others. Being a peacemaker means first looking in our heart and asking ourselves: "How do I treat others, especially those who are different from me? Am I treating them as Jesus would?" Then we have to look at how our society treats others and, as Christians, work toward changing unjust institutions or laws.

Cooperative Thumb Wrestling

Paired Activity (10 minutes)

This activity demonstrates that we often compete, even when it is against our best interest.

1. Have the teens choose a partner and get into thumb-wrestling position (interlocked fingers with thumbs pointing up). Do not, however, use the term *thumb wrestling,* because it denotes competition. If teens use the term, explain that the position is the same, but the rules are different. Give the pairs these instructions:

- The goal of this activity is to accumulate as many points as possible. A point is accumulated when one partner covers the thumb of the other partner with his or her own thumb. The following rules apply to this activity:
  ○ You may not talk.
  ○ You must keep track of your own points. Each point will be worth one thousand dollars.

2. Say, "Begin!" and allow 30 seconds of play. The partners will invariably compete. Stop the game after 30 seconds. Invite the players to say aloud the number of points they earned. Then lead a discussion with the whole group based on the following questions:

- Why did you automatically compete?
- What was the goal of the game?
  Next, say something like this:
- The goal of the game was to accumulate as many points as possible, not to see which individual would score the most points. If you could play the game over again, what could you do differently to achieve the goal?

  If the teens cannot come up with an answer, explain that they could cooperate—with each partner taking turns putting his or her own thumb over the thumb of his or her partner, and they could use both pairs of hands at the same time.

3. Play the game again for 15 seconds, this time allowing the partners to work cooperatively. Then stop and ask each pair the total number of points accumulated this time. Usually it is far greater than when they competed. Continue by sharing the following information in your own words:

- When this game is played, the highest number of points scored by a single person in the first round is typically no more than a dozen. When the pairs work cooperatively, as in the second round, some teams have scored over one hundred points. In terms of money, in the first round the most a person would make would be twelve thousand dollars, and in the second round, one hundred thousand dollars.

   Stimulate discussion by posing the following questions to the whole group:
- Did the other person's gaining points mean that you lost points?
- What did you stand to gain by cooperation?
- How many would still rather be declared the sole "winner" with twelve points than share the win with another person for one hundred points? Why?
- In what other situations do people compete without thinking?
- What does this game say about being peacemakers?
- Can you cite examples of when Jesus used cooperation rather than competition?

4. Make the following points in your own words:
- I am not saying that individual achievement should be eliminated from life. We enjoy seeing people excel; that is why the Olympics are so popular. However, cooperation as a possible way of living is something that has not been truly appreciated by our society. Cooperation is a very Christian way of living. This game has shown that we gain so much more by cooperating than by competing.

5. Call for two volunteers. Ask each volunteer to read one of the following Scripture passages: Mark 9:33–35 and James 3:16—4:3.

   Conclude by asking the whole group how these passages relate to the activity and discussion.

Break (10 minutes)

Anytown U.S.A.

Small-Group Activity (60–75 minutes)
The purpose of Anytown U.S.A. is to expose teens to the disparities in our society and to empower them to make changes to improve our world.

Materials Needed

☐ one copy of resource 3–A, "Company Descriptions," cut apart
☐ a scissors
☐ six blindfolds
☐ a ball of string
☐ masking tape
☐ $750 of play money, photocopied from resource 3–B, "Money"
☐ *optional:* a poster for each month containing the task instruction for that month (see the directions for each month)
☐ scratch paper and pencils
☐ three Bibles

Before the retreat, be sure to acquire and prepare the necessary materials. Resource 3–A, "Company Descriptions," provides a description of each company, assigns disabilities to each company, and specifies the amount of equity each company is to receive. Photocopy and cut apart this resource and resource 3–B, "Money." You will need three small groups. Determine who should be in each group. Then assign a disability to certain people in each group by filling in their names in the blanks on resource 3–A. You may need to adjust the disability assignments on the resource based on the number of people in each small group. Ensure that at least one person in each group does not have a disability.

The game is played over a fictional four- to five-month period. Each month lasts approximately 15 minutes in real time.

Explain the game to the group along the following lines:

- You are all citizens of Anytown, U.S.A.; the town is so named because it could exist anywhere in the United States. Anytown has three major companies that employ the townspeople. Each family in Anytown has at least one member working for one of these companies.

    The three companies are Bill Gatesorama High Tech Company, which produces some of the best computer products in the country; Harvard Educational Company, which trains all teachers who teach in the school system and has a reputation for training some of the best teachers in the country; and Leona's Hotel and Quality Service Control Company, which owns and operates all the leading hotels, restaurants, and dance clubs in Anytown.

    You will be divided into three small groups representing the employees of each of the companies. I, the retreat director, am the mayor. After you have been placed in your small group, you will be given more information about your company.

    Each group must select one person to be the boss. This person will receive all the instructions. You must also choose two employees to be members of the town council. At the end of months two, three, four, and five, the town council meets to accomplish these tasks:
    ○ Discuss the rules of the town and determine whether any rules need to be changed.
    ○ Discuss ways to assist any company that is on probation.
    ○ Discuss how to spend the town's community trust fund money.

    The ultimate *goal* of the council is to keep everyone employed and to improve life for *all* the citizens of Anytown.

    At the beginning of every month, each company will donate $25 to the community trust fund, which will be used by the town for emergencies. The money cannot be used to get a company off probation. Each month the three companies compete for contracts from various groups. The company that comes in first receives the contract and a $50 bonus, the company that comes in second receives a $25 bonus, and the company that comes in last receives nothing. This money represents your company's income, which pays the employees' salaries.

If at the end of the second month a company has not received any contracts or is out of money, that company is on probation and cannot compete for contracts. In order to get off probation, the company must pay a $50 fee. This fee is not negotiable and cannot be changed even by the town council, but the council can change other rules in order to help all the companies. While a company is on probation, the other companies must each put an additional $25 into the community trust fund.

Give the teens their company assignments. Have each small group select its boss and two town council members. Remind the young people that the town council members represent all the employees of their company, and their role is to keep everyone employed and to improve life for all the citizens of Anytown.

Give each group its company description from resource 3–A, the materials needed for its disabilities (blindfolds, string, tape), and its designated amount of play money.

Begin the game. Have each group sit in its own circle on the floor, apart from the other groups.

Month 1

Collect the $25 community trust fund money from each company. Post the following task instruction for month 1. Make sure all the groups can see the poster at the same time. (If you don't want to use a poster, simply read the task instruction aloud to the groups.)

- The Macintosh Math and Science Center is submitting its contract to the company that can best perform addition calculations. When given the signal to begin, a disabled employee must calculate the total number of years your group has been alive by writing down the figures, adding them up, and then giving them to the mayor.

After determining first and second place, award the first-place company $50 and the second-place company $25.

Wait until the end of month 2 to hold a town council meeting. The teens need time to get into the game.

Month 2

Collect the $25 community trust fund money from each company. Post or read aloud the following task instruction for month 2:

- The Performing Arts Council is submitting its contract to the company that can sing the best. When given the signal to begin, your group must stand and move in a circle while singing "Jingle Bells." The company showing the most enthusiasm and with the most number of people singing will come in first place and win the contract.

After determining first and second place, award the first-place company $50 and the second-place company $25.

If any company is on probation, collect the extra $25 from the remaining companies and put the money into the community trust fund.

Next, prepare to hold a town council meeting in front of all the small groups. Explain that during the meeting only the town council members may speak and make decisions. Thus, before the meeting, allow time for the small groups to discuss amongst themselves any changes they would like to see in the rules of the game or any other suggestions they have for improving life in Anytown. The town council members may do the following during the meeting:

- Discuss the rules of the town (i.e., community trust fund, how contracts are awarded, conditions of their employees) and determine whether any changes are needed to improve life for all the citizens of Anytown.
- If any company is on probation, discuss ways to assist that company.
- Decide whether to spend any community trust fund money. [Explain to the town council that they have to decide whether to spend the community trust fund money right away or save it. Some may want to buy things to make life better, such as seeing-eye dogs for their blind employees. As the mayor, use your discretion to set a price for each item, such as $50 for the dogs.]

After coming to any decisions during the council meeting, the council members must go back to their company and get final permission from the other employees to approve any changes that were discussed. If the other employees do not agree, then any change is null and void.

Allow time for the representatives to discuss the town council's decisions with their company employees. Ask one of the representatives to read aloud the various decisions discussed. After each decision is read, call for a show of hands from all the employees to approve it. Any decision that is not unanimous does not get passed.

Month 3

Collect the $25 community trust fund money from each company (unless the town council has changed this rule). Post the following task instruction for month 3:

- The Nikkey Sports Commission is submitting its contract for the company whose employees can run the fastest. When given the signal to begin, the employees of your company must lock arms with one another and run to the other end of the room, tag the wall, and return. The first company to complete the task wins the contract.

After determining first and second place, award the first-place company $50 and the second-place company $25 (unless the town council has changed this rule).

If any company is on probation, collect the extra $25 from the remaining companies and put the money into the community trust fund.

Hold a town council meeting. Repeat the directions for the meeting as given in month 2.

Month 4

Collect the $25 community trust fund money from each company (unless the town council has changed this rule). Give each company a Bible. Post or read aloud the following task instruction for month 4:

- The Faithfully Redeemed–Already Saved Church is submitting its contract to the company that can best quote the Scriptures. When given the signal to begin, your small group must open its Bible to Matthew 25:40 and have all members memorize the passage in order to say it aloud together. The first company to call over the mayor and accurately quote the Scripture passage aloud together wins the contract. The second company to call over the mayor and accurately quote the Scripture passage aloud wins the $25 bonus.

After determining first and second place, award the first-place company $50 and the second-place company $25 (unless the town council has changed this rule).

If any company is on probation, collect the extra $25 from the remaining companies and put the money into the community trust fund.

Hold a town council meeting. Repeat the directions for the meeting as given in month 2, with the addition of the following complication:

Two minutes into the town council meeting, announce to the council that you have just received an emergency bulletin. Read this aloud to the council:

- A tornado just ripped through town and destroyed the roof on the high school. It will cost $200 to fix. If the roof is not fixed, then the high school students will have to go to school during the summer in the grade school building. Also, a toxic waste site was just discovered and has to be cleaned up immediately. This will cost $200. If it is not cleaned up, the whole town will develop cancer within a year. To pay for both of these emergencies, we will have to take money from the community trust fund.

Allow another 3 minutes for the council meeting and then go through the voting procedure as usual.

Month 5

Collect the $25 community trust fund money from each company (unless the town council has changed this rule). Post or read aloud the following task instruction for month 5:

- The Pablo Picassogoya Gallery is submitting its contract to the company that can draw the best. When given the signal to begin, one blind person in your group must draw a picture depicting all the members of your small group and what they are wearing. The first company to complete the task wins the contract.

After determining first and second place, award the first-place company $50 and the second-place company $25 (unless the town council has changed this rule).

If any company is on probation, collect the extra $25 from the remaining companies and put the money into the community trust fund.

Hold a town council meeting. Repeat the directions for the meeting as given in month 2.

After the last month, lead a discussion with the whole group based on the following questions:
- Was the goal of the game—keeping people employed and improving life for all the citizens of Anytown—achieved? Why or why not?
- Was the game fair? Why or why not?
- How did you feel during the game?
- Did any of your own actions or reactions surprise you? How?
- Did any actions or reactions of the other players surprise you? How?
- In what ways did people behave as people would likely behave in real life?
- In what ways was it easy to negotiate changes during the town council meetings? What would have made it easier?
- Were the lives of *all* the citizens improved as a result of your decisions? How?
- Were there any unjust structures or conditions in the game? Did anyone really benefit from these? How?
- What is our responsibility as Christians to other members of our society?
- How would Jesus respond to the previous question?

Lunch (45 minutes)

Icebreakers (15 minutes)
Choose from among the icebreakers offered in part A of the appendix of this book, or use games of your own.

Lazarus Skit Large-Group Activity (15–30 minutes)
In this activity the teens reflect on the Gospel mandate Jesus gave us to serve poor people.

Before the retreat be sure to make at least four copies of the skit found on resource 3–C, "Lazarus and the Rich Man." You may also want to put together some props to make the skit more fun. Here are some suggestions:
- *For the Narrator.* A fake microphone
- *For the Rich Man.* A suit jacket, a top hat, some fake jewelry
- *For Lazarus.* A shirt with a lot of patches, pants with a hole in the knee
- *For Abraham.* A long white robe
- *For the Angels.* Halos or sets of wings

Call for four volunteers to help act out the story of the rich man and Lazarus. Assign one of the following parts to each volunteer: Narrator, Rich Man, Lazarus, Abraham. If you want to include more teens, you can have several angels as non-speaking parts.

Direct the volunteers to act out the skit of Lazarus and the Rich Man. Following the skit, discuss these questions with the whole group:
- What decision did the Rich Man make?
- How do you react when someone approaches you on the street and asks for money?

- What is the message Jesus wanted to communicate to the listeners of this story?
- Can being rich be an obstacle for someone who is trying to follow Jesus?

Read the following statistics to the whole group:

- One in four U.S. children lives in poverty—double the child poverty rate of any other industrialized country.
- Thirty-eight million people in the United States live in poverty—a million more than in 1994.
- In 1973 the average income of the richest fifth of the U.S. population was seven times that of the poorest fifth. Today the income of the richest fifth is over 10.5 times the income of the poorest fifth.

(Bread for the World Annual Report 1995)

- In the United States, 2,699 infants are born into poverty every day.
- In the United States, 27 children—a classroom full—die because of poverty every day.
- Every day in the United States, 95 babies die before their first birthday.
- Every day in the United States, 100,000 children are homeless.

(Children's Defense Fund,
The State of America's Children Yearbook 1995)

- The average decline in women's standard of living the first year of divorce is 26 percent.
- The average increase in men's standard of living the first year after divorce is 34 percent.
- The number of parents who receive only partial or none of awarded child support is 51 percent.

(Women's Legal Defense Fund, University of Denver, U.S. Census
Bureau, National Center for Health Statistics)

Conclude the activity by posing these questions to the whole group:
- Is it easy or difficult to believe these statistics? Why?
- How, as Christians, can we respond to these statistics?

Charitable Small-Group Activity (15–20 minutes)

The purpose of this activity is for the teens to consider biblical examples of people putting others first.

1. Form small groups. Give each group a Bible. Assign each small group one of the following Scripture passages:
- John 6:1–14
- Mark 3:1–6
- Luke 10:30–37
- John 13:5–15
- Matt. 5:38–45
- Luke 23:33–34

Instruct the teens using words similar to the following:

• Let's take a look at some examples from the Scriptures of people who were able to put the needs of others ahead of their own. Each small group has been assigned a Scripture passage. Your group's job is to read the passage and design a pantomime (silent skit) depicting the story. After each small group performs its pantomime, the other small groups will try to guess what Scripture saying, event, or story it depicts.

2. Give the teams several minutes to prepare. Then have them take turns presenting their pantomime. After each pantomime, invite the whole group to guess what saying, event, or story the team is acting out.

3. After all the pantomimes have been presented, discuss the passages with the whole group using the following questions:

• Who put themselves last and others first in each Scripture passage? Why did they do it?
• What did the person risk by doing this? What were her or his rewards?

Works of Mercy **Small-Group Activity (20 minutes)**
This activity encourages the teens to think of ways they could perform the works of mercy.

Post a banner with the following works of mercy printed on it:

• Feed the hungry.
• Give drink to the thirsty.
• Clothe the naked.
• Visit the sick.
• Shelter the homeless.
• Visit the imprisoned.
• Bury the dead.
• Pray for the living and the dead.

Read the works of mercy aloud to the whole group and brainstorm with them how these works can be used in their home, school, and community.

Then offer these instructions in your own words:

• I am going to assign one of the works of mercy to each small group. Your small group is to take the verb from each phrase, for example, *feed* in "Feed the hungry," and write each letter of the verb on a separate piece of paper. Then your group is to come up with an action step beginning with each letter that would illustrate how someone could live out that particular work of mercy.

Give the following example for "Feed the hungry":

• Find a soup kitchen and volunteer.
• Eat less so that there is more for others.
• Educate others to the real problem of world hunger.
• Donate canned goods to a local food pantry.

When the groups are finished, have them tape their verbs together and share their action steps with the whole group.

Classified Ad   **Affirmation (15–20 minutes)**
In this activity the teens validate their own gifts and talents.

Give everyone a piece of paper and a pencil. Then explain these directions:

- In this activity you will each write a classified ad about yourself. Classified ads found in the newspaper are typically short in length and describe items and services to be offered. You are to use this concept to write your own ad. Include in your ad your name and any characteristics that make you special and unique. This can include physical attributes (such as height and eye color), internal qualities (such as good listener, adventurous), and any hobbies and talents you possess.

Give the young people enough time to complete their ad. Then invite each person to read his or her ad either to fellow small-group members or to the whole group.

Peace Revisited   **Large-Group Brainstorming (10 minutes)**
In this activity the teens see if their opinions about peace have changed since the beginning of the retreat.

Post the list of words and images of peace that the group brainstormed at the beginning of the retreat. Invite the retreatants to call out any new words or images that come to their mind now when they hear the word *peace.*

After this second brainstorming session, compare the new list with the original list. Point out any changes in attitudes that might have surfaced.

Call for a volunteer to write a definition of peace based on the words from both lists.

**Closing Guided
Meditation**   **(20–30 minutes)**
Begin the meditation with a progressive muscle relaxation exercise (see part C of the appendix for suggestions). If possible, play soft instrumental background music. Then continue with the following guided meditation. Pause for a few seconds at each ellipsis (. . .).

- There are many places in our world where peace does not exist. Jesus reminds us that peace is possible, but we have to work for it. Many people through the ages have worked to relieve suffering and bring justice to disadvantaged people. We are called to do the same, knowing that God is always there to guide and support us.

Imagine you are back in the time when Jesus lived on earth. . . . You are in the upper room with the disciples. . . . You have just finished eating the Passover meal. . . . Everyone is seated around a table and seems very excited. . . . This is a very special feast—a celebration of the liberation that occurred when Moses led the Israelites out of slavery. . . .

Look around the room. . . . See the reflections on the wall from the candles. . . . Smell the various foods that have just been eaten. . . .

Now Jesus gets up and takes a bowl of water and a towel. He goes first to Saint Peter to wash his feet. . . . Saint Peter seems annoyed or embarrassed and says, "Jesus, are you going to wash my feet?" . . .

Jesus answers, "You don't understand now what I am doing, but you will understand later." . . .

Peter remarks, "No, you will never wash my feet." . . .

Jesus answers, "If I don't wash your feet, you are not one of my people." . . .

Peter lets Jesus wash his feet. . . . Jesus goes around the table washing the feet of all the disciples. . . .

Now he comes to you, to wash your feet. . . . How do you feel right now? [Longer pause.] What do you want to say to Jesus? Spend some time sharing with Jesus now. [Longer pause.]

After Jesus washes your feet, he asks you to name ways in which you have been a peacemaker in your family [longer pause], in your school [longer pause], in your community [longer pause].

Jesus then asks you to name ways in which you have fallen short of being a peacemaker. [Longer pause.] What sometimes prevents you from being a peacemaker? [Longer pause.] What do you need in order to be a peacemaker in the future, and how can Jesus help you? [Longer pause.] What's one quality you have that helps you to be God's instrument of peace? [Longer pause.] What's one thing you would like to do but have been afraid of doing? [Longer pause.]

Jesus tells you that not everyone understood what he was trying to do, and that being a peacemaker isn't always easy but it's very rewarding. . . .

Before Jesus goes he asks you if there's anything else you want to talk with him about. . . . Spend these last few minutes talking with Jesus or just sitting quietly with him. [Longer pause.]

Jesus gives you a sign of peace and then leaves the room. . . . You are now the only one left, and you decide to say a prayer: "Dear Jesus, thank you for your example of peacemaking. Give me the strength to follow your example, especially when people do not understand why I do what I do. Give me peace in my heart so that I can bring peace to all those around me. Amen."

When you open your eyes, you will no longer be back in time but here in this room. When you are ready, slowly open your eyes and come back.

Evaluation

Large Group (5 minutes)

After the guided meditation, direct the teens to reflect in writing on the following questions. Invite them to answer aloud if they feel comfortable doing so.

- If you had only one word to describe today, what word would you pick?
- What is one new thing you learned today, or what is one thing you really liked? (It might be something we did or something someone said.)
- What do you feel God is challenging you to do as a result of this retreat?

Company Descriptions

Cut this resource apart along the dashed lines.

Bill Gatesorama High Tech Company

Your company produces some of the best computer products in the country. You, the employees, receive a decent wage. Each month your company gets a bonus if it has won new contracts. Therefore, you work very hard at coming in first each month in order to secure these contracts. If after the second month your company has received no contracts or is out of money, you are on probation and cannot compete for contracts until your company has paid a fee of $50.

Your company does not discriminate in its hiring practices. Thus your company has one blind employee (who wears a blindfold) and one physically disabled employee (who has his or her feet bound with string)

Right now your company has $175 in equity.

blind employee _____

disabled employee _____

Harvard Educational Company

Your center trains all the teachers who teach in the school system. You have an established reputation for training and hiring some of the best teachers in the country. You, the employees, receive a decent wage. Each month your company gets a bonus if it has won new contracts. Therefore, you work very hard at coming in first each month in order to secure these contracts. If after the second month your company has received no contracts or is out of money, you are on probation and cannot compete for contracts until your company has paid a fee of $50.

Your company does not discriminate in its hiring practices. Thus your company has two blind employees (who wear blindfolds), one physically disabled employee (who has his or her feet bound with string), and one mute employee (whose mouth has masking tape over it).

Right now your company has $125 in equity.

blind employees _____ _____

disabled employee _____

mute employee _____

Leona's Hotel and Quality Service Control Company

Your company owns and operates all the leading hotels, restaurants, and dance clubs in town. You, the employees, receive a decent wage. Each month your company gets a bonus if it has won new contracts. Therefore, you work very hard at coming in first each month in order to secure these contracts. If after the second month your company has received no contracts or is out of money, you are on probation and cannot compete for contracts until your company has paid a fee of $50.

Your company does not discriminate in its hiring practices. Thus your company has three blind employees (who wear blindfolds), three physically disabled employees (who have their hands and feet tied with string), and three mute employees (whose mouths have masking tape over them).

Right now your company has $50 in equity.

blind employees _____ _____ _____

disabled employees _____ _____ _____

mute employees _____ _____ _____

Money

Make enough copies of this resource to equal $750 of play money. Cut the money apart.

Lazarus and the Rich Man

Narrator. Once upon a time there was a very, very, very . . . I mean obscenely rich guy. We will just call him the Rich Man. There was also a really, really, really . . . I mean terribly poor guy named Lazarus. Here's their story.

　　The Rich Man always dressed in the finest clothes and lived in luxury every day. The very poor man named Lazarus had sores covering his whole body. He sat at the Rich Man's gate. Lazarus cried out:

Lazarus. Oh please, Mr. Rich Man, can't you spare some extra food for me? I am soooooooooo hungry. All I want are your leftovers.

Narrator. Lazarus wasn't looking for a big meal (although he really needed one). He wanted to eat only the small pieces of food that fell from the Rich Man's table.

Rich Man. Well then, what will my pets eat if I give you the leftovers?

Narrator. So poor Lazarus didn't get any help from the Rich Man. Later, Lazarus died, and the angels carried him to the arms of Abraham. The Rich Man died, too, and was buried. But the Rich Man was not very happy. Actually, he was now in a lot of pain. The Rich Man saw Abraham far away (you know, up in heaven) with Lazarus at his side and called:

Rich Man. Father Abraham, have mercy on me! Send Lazarus to dip his finger in water and cool my tongue, because I am suffering in this fire (you know, hell).

Narrator. Obviously the Rich Man has not learned his lesson. He still thinks Lazarus is beneath him and should serve him. Well, is he ever wrong!

Abraham. Child, remember when you were alive you had all the good things, but bad things happened to Lazarus? And you didn't help him. Now Lazarus is comforted here, and you are suffering. Besides, there is a big pit between you and us, so no one can cross over to you, and no one can leave there and come here.

Rich Man. Father Abraham, then please send Lazarus to my house on earth. I have five brothers, and Lazarus could warn them so that they will not come to this place of pain (you know, hell).

Narrator. He's still out of touch!

Abraham. Your brothers have the Law of Moses and the writing of the prophets. They have been taught right from wrong.

Rich Man. No, Father Abraham. They are stubborn like me. If they saw a miracle—someone coming back from the dead—then they would believe and change their hearts and lives.

Abraham. If they will not listen to Moses and the prophets, then they will not listen to someone who has come back from the dead.

(Adapted from Luke 16:19–31)

Retreat 4

Prayer
and Our Relationship
with Jesus

Theme
This retreat encourages teens to reflect on their personal relationship with Jesus and to examine different styles of prayer as a way to enrich this relationship.

Bible Basis
John 6:5–14. In the story of Jesus feeding the five thousand, we realize that Jesus does in fact change our life if we let him. Through faith and prayer, our relationship with Jesus can grow, change, and be strengthened.

Objectives
The retreatants will do the following:
- be challenged to grow into a deeper relationship with Jesus
- examine some of the relationships Jesus had with people during his lifetime
- learn about the qualities of a healthy friendship and discuss the importance of friends in our life
- experience various forms of prayer
- be encouraged to develop a deeper appreciation for prayer as a way to enrich one's relationship with Jesus

Retreat at a Glance

The following chart offers a brief overview of the retreat activities, time frames, and materials needed. For more detailed information about any of the activities, refer to the directions given in the Retreat in Detail section.

ACTIVITY	TIME FRAME	SUPPLIES
Welcome and Introduction	10–15 minutes	poster with standards
Icebreakers	15–30 minutes	depends on selection
Opening Prayer	5 minutes	Bible
What Is Friendship?	15–20 minutes	pipe cleaners
Jesus Relay	25–30 minutes	newsprint, markers, masking tape
Jesus Changes Things	15–25 minutes	Bible, handout 4–A, pencils, newsprint, marker
Break	10 minutes	
Trust	15–20 minutes	
Friends of Jesus	15–25 minutes	Bibles, newsprint, markers
Lunch	45 minutes	
Icebreakers	15 minutes	depends on selection
Prayer Statistics	15 minutes	paper, marker, masking tape
The Power of Prayer	30 minutes	resource 4–A, scissors, masking tape, Bibles, index cards, pencils
PRAY	15 minutes	newsprint, markers, masking tape
Anonymous Affirmations	20 minutes	index cards, pencils, basket
Closing Prayer	55–75 minutes	handout 4–B, handout booklets, pencils, cassette tapes, cassette player
Evaluation	5 minutes	pencils, paper

Retreat in Detail

Welcome and Introduction

(10–15 minutes)

Icebreakers

(15–30 minutes)
Choose from among the icebreakers offered in part A of the appendix of this book, or use games of your own.

Opening Prayer

(5 minutes)
Begin the prayer by reading aloud John 6:5–14, the account of the multiplication of the loaves and fishes. Finish with a prayer similar to this one:
- Dear God, just as you changed the bread and fish into enough food for everyone, please continue to change and remold us. Like the disciples, we, too, can be skeptical and fearful of others and of situations that seem beyond our control. Help us to be open to the many miracles around us each day. Teach us to pray constantly so that our life may be richer and more connected to you. The large crowd of people who came to hear you preach and to be healed truly believed in you and your ability to transform them. Give us that faith, developed through prayer and our friendship with you. Amen.

What Is Friendship?

Small-Group Activity (15–20 minutes)
The purpose of this activity is for the teens to discuss the various qualities of friendship.

1. Arrange the teens in small groups and give each person one pipe cleaner. Then offer the following directions in your own words:
- Think of a really good friend you have. Picture this person in your imagination. What is it about this person that makes him or her such a good friend? What qualities do you admire in this person?
Give everyone time to think. Then continue:
- Without saying who your friend is, tell the other small-group members about your friend's qualities. Let's have the person in each group with the smallest shoe size begin.

2. When the groups are finished, continue with these directions:
- Now, using only pipe cleaners, create your group's symbol of friendship. Think about the qualities you just discussed, and pick the one your group believes is the most important. All members must agree on the quality and the symbol. For example, you could create a phone to illustrate a good listener. Make sure each person in your group helps with this project. Your group will need a reporter, someone to explain your group's symbol. Let's have the reporter be the person in each group with the longest first name.
   Allow a few minutes for the groups to create their symbols. Then invite each reporter to describe what her or his group created.

3. Lead a large-group discussion using the following questions (see the introduction for alternative ways of debriefing this and other retreat activities):

- What did you like about this activity? Why? What did you dislike? Why?
- How did you feel about working together in your small group to create these symbols of friendship?
- How was working on this project similar to the process of developing a friendship?
- What new things did you learn about the people in your small group through working together on this activity?
- How do you define the word *friendship?*
- How do you develop friendships?

4. Conclude the activity by saying something like this:
- A friendship can be created in many ways. One of the most important ingredients is spending time with each other and doing things together. By spending time together, you can learn a lot about another person, about yourself, and about the kind of friend you are. Today we will work together to examine our relationship with Jesus, and we will explore prayer as a way of deepening that relationship.

Jesus Relay

Small-Group Activity (25–30 minutes)

In this activity the retreatants identify the many characteristics of Jesus.

1. Form small groups and ask them to line up in rows on one side of the room. On the opposite side of the room, have tables set up with a sheet of newsprint and a marker for each group. Give the following directions to the whole group:
- We are going to brainstorm about the name *Jesus.* The object of this exercise is to come up with as many words or images of Jesus as possible. To do that, we will have a relay race. Each person will have several chances to run over to the table, write on the newsprint a word or image they associate with Jesus, and then run back and tag his or her teammate, who will run over and do the same. You cannot repeat any word or image that someone in your group has already written. The team with the longest list of words or images wins. You have 3 minutes. Go.

2. After 3 minutes call time and have all the small groups sit down. Continue by saying something like this:
- Your small group needs a reporter for the next part of this exercise. Let's have the person in each group with the shortest first name be the reporter. Review your newsprint list to make sure you understand all the words and images on it. Count the number of words and images. Write that number somewhere on the newsprint and circle it.

    Invite the reporters to come up to the front of the room one at a time and share their group's words or images. Hang up the sheets of newsprint with masking tape.

3. Start a discussion with the whole group by raising the following questions:
- Was it easy or difficult to think of different descriptions of Jesus? Why?

- Were you surprised by any of the words and images your group came up with? Which ones?
- Can you think of other words and images that we all forgot?
- How did you come to know about these words and images of Jesus?
- How does your relationship with Jesus affect your understanding of his identity?

4. Offer a conclusion like the following:

- It's good to know things about another person. With our friends, it helps us to see what we have in common. Yet it's not enough just to know things *about* our friends, we need to know them. That can only happen by spending time with them, sharing with them—in essence, having a relationship with them. The same is true of Jesus. We hope to share what we know about Jesus, as well as to work on our relationship with him.

Jesus Changes Things

Small-Group Activity (15–25 minutes)

The purpose of this activity is to make the teens aware that Jesus can change many things in our life if we let him.

1. Call for a volunteer to read aloud John 6:5–14. Then give each person a copy of handout 4–A, "Jesus Changes Things," and a pencil. Read the directions on the handout aloud to the teens.

   Put the sample puzzle problem on newsprint and go through it, demonstrating the process.

   Give the small groups 15 minutes to work on solving as many of the puzzle problems as possible. The solutions to the puzzles can be found on the page facing the handout. Do not photocopy and distribute the answer key.

2. When time is up, invite one person from each small group to share which puzzles his or her group was able to figure out and how the group figured them out.

   Lead a discussion with the whole group using the following questions:

- Was this exercise easy or difficult? Why?
- What are the benefits of change? What are the disadvantages?
- Why do people resist change?
- How does Jesus change things today?

   (Adapted from Finley, *Good Clean Fun,* vol. 2, p. 60)

3. Conclude the activity by conveying this information in your own words:

- When we talk about Jesus, we are talking about a personal relationship. And all relationships grow and go through changes. The first major change Jesus went through was the Incarnation. God loved us so much and wanted to have a personal relationship with us so much that Jesus became human. God knew it would be difficult to have a relationship with someone you cannot see or relate to. So God conceived his Son, Jesus, to be born as one of us. Today we don't have Jesus living as a human with us, but that doesn't mean we can't have a relationship with him. Like any relationship, we have to work at it for it to continue.

At this time you may wish to share a personal story about how your relationship with Jesus has changed and grown over your lifetime, and how you work on your relationship with Jesus. Name some things you do to keep that relationship alive and growing.

Break (10 minutes)

Trust Large-Group Activity (15–20 minutes)

This activity helps the teens appreciate that trust is an essential element of a strong relationship.

1. Introduce the activity this way:
- The name of this first game is the Yurt Circle. The name comes from the ingenious Mongolian nomads' tent where the roof pushes against the walls in perfect equilibrium, keeping the structure standing.

2. Direct the whole group to stand and form a circle (you need an even number of people). All face the center, standing almost shoulder to shoulder and holding hands. Then have one person say, "In," the next person say, "Out," and so on until everyone around the entire circle has responded. Then give the whole group these instructions:
- On the count of three, the "Ins" will lean toward the center of the circle while the "Outs" lean back. We must all keep our feet stationary and support ourselves with our held hands. With a bit of practice, we should be able to lean amazingly far forward and backward without falling. Once our yurt is stable, we will count to three and try having the "Ins" and the "Outs" switch roles while we continue holding hands.

(Adapted from Fluegelman, *More New Games!* p. 123)

3. After the first exercise, continue with the next trust activity called the Lap game. Have everyone stand in a circle again, shoulder to shoulder. Instruct the teens to turn to the right and very gently sit down on the lap of the person behind them. If the group is really good, they can start to walk around in a circle while seated, or all try waving their hands.

(Based on Fluegelman, ed., *The New Games Book,* p. 171)

4. Following the two trust exercises, discuss these questions as a group:
- Was trust required to achieve success in these games? How?
- Why is it important to trust our friends?
- What makes it hard for us to trust?
- How do we regain trust after it has been lost?
- What makes it easy or hard to trust Jesus?

Friends of Jesus Small-Group Activity (15–25 minutes)

The purpose of this activity is for the teens to have the opportunity to identify with people whom the Scriptures depict as friends of Jesus.

1. Form small groups. Give each small group a sheet of newsprint and a marker. Explain this introduction to the activity in your own words:

• The Christian Testament serves as a record of the many friendships Jesus had. Your small group will get a chance to look at one of Jesus' friendships and discuss it. Then you will share your reflections with the other small groups. For this exercise your group will need a reader to read the Scripture passage, a recorder to write down your group's answers, and a reporter to share your group's answers aloud. Let's have the reader be the person in each group whose birthday is closest to today's date, the recorder be the person whose birthday is closest to Christmas, and the reporter be the person whose birthday is closest to Valentine's Day.

2. Write the following questions on newsprint and display them for all to see:

• What happened to the person in your assigned story as a result of his or her encounter with Jesus?
• Pretend you are the person in the story. What feelings do you have toward Jesus? What would you have said to Jesus?
• Compare the story of this relationship with a personal experience of your own.

Use the person of Zacchaeus as an example. Call for a volunteer to read Luke 19:1–9. Have the whole group help you answer the first two questions. Answer the third question yourself, sharing a personal story of how the passage relates to your life. This will help the teens understand what is expected of them.

3. Assign a different person from the Scriptures to each small group. Choose from the following, or add some of your own:

• *Peter.* Matt. 26:69–75; John 21:15–19
• *John the Baptist.* Mark 1:4–8; Matt. 3:13–15
• *Mary Magdalene.* Luke 7:36–50; John 20:11–18
• *Judas Iscariot.* John 13:21–30; John 18:1–9
• *Andrew.* Matt 4:18–20; Matt. 10:1–15
• *Matthew (Levi).* Matt. 9:9–13; Luke 5:27–32
• *Nicodemus.* John 3:1–21; 19:38–42
• *Thomas.* John 14:1–14; 20:24–29

4. When all are finished, encourage the reporters to share their small group's answers with the whole group. Also, if you have time, direct the small groups to develop a role-play about their assigned person and his or her relationship with Jesus.

Lunch (45 minutes)

Icebreakers (15 minutes)

Choose from among the icebreakers offered in part A of the appendix of this book, or use games of your own.

Prayer Statistics

Large-Group Activity (15 minutes)

In this activity the retreatants compare their faith and prayer beliefs with those of other teens.

Label each of ten sheets of paper with a different percentage in increments of ten up to 100. Tape the sheets of paper about 3 feet apart on the floor. Give the group the following instructions:

- Christian teenagers from around the United States were surveyed about their faith and prayer life. I'm going to read the survey questions they responded to, and I want you to guess what percentage of the teen population answered yes to those questions. On the floor are numbers from 10 percent to 100 percent. Stand by the population percentage that you believe is closest to the correct answer.

Read the statements aloud, one at a time. After each statement, give the teens time to move. Then ask them to explain their choice. After several teens have answered, call out the correct percentage and then proceed with the next statement.

- The young people surveyed attend church and/or their youth group at least three times a month. [90 percent]
- They feel it's important to tell (or show) others about their faith in Christ. [70 percent]
- They spend time in prayer every day. [50 percent]
- They say their Christian beliefs greatly influence their daily decisions. [40 percent]
- They spend time reading the Bible every day. [20 percent]
  (Statistics from "What Really Impacts Kids' Spiritual Growth," *Group Inside*, p. 21; percentages were rounded off)
- They say they believe in God or a universal spirit. [100 percent]
- They believe in life after death. [70 percent]
- They believe life really matters and has meaning. [90 percent]
  (Statistics from Woods, *What's A Christian?* p. 4; percentages were rounded off)

At the end of the activity, discuss the following questions with the group:

- Did any of the statistics surprise you? If so, why?
- Which statistic was the most significant to you? Why?
- What is the power of prayer?

You may want to share the following story, or a similar one, and ask if the teens have stories about the power of prayer in their own life or the life of someone they know.

- In an experiment at San Francisco General Hospital, reported in the Southern Medical Journal, a researcher asked outsiders to pray for a group of cardiac patients. Even though the patients weren't told that prayers were being said for them, the study found that they recovered faster than those in an otherwise identical control group. ("Bringing God into the World," *Newsweek*)

The Power of Prayer

Large-Group Activity (30 minutes)

In this activity the teens explore why they do or do not believe in the power of prayer.

Before the retreat, make several copies of resource 4–A, "Prayer Quotes," and cut them apart on the dashed lines. Tape the quotes on the walls all over your meeting room. It's okay to have the same quote posted in more than one place.

1. Direct the teens to form a circle with their chairs in the middle of the room. Tell everyone to sit facing away from the center of the circle. Explain the activity this way:
- Now we are going to examine the idea of prayer. Posted all around the room are quotes expressing a variety of perspectives on prayer. You have 3 minutes to examine the quotes and carry back to the circle the quote that best expresses the way you feel about prayer. Ready? Go.

2. When everyone has chosen a quote, have the teens gather near you. Tell everyone to toss their chosen quote into a pile. One by one, select a quote from the pile and read it aloud. After each quote, say:
- If you agree with this quote, move to my left. If you disagree with it, move to my right.

    Wait for the teens to respond, then ask a few people from each group to defend their choice.

3. After going through several quotes, gather the teens back in the circle with their chairs facing in, and lead a discussion based on the following questions:
- Why do people pray or not pray?
- What power does prayer have?
- Was there a time when you knew for sure that God answered one of your prayers? If so, when?
- Was there a time when you prayed but nothing happened? If so, when?
- How do you know God has answered a prayer if the answer is not yes?
- Why and when are you most likely to pray?
- Why and when are you most likely not to pray?

4. Have the teens form small groups. Give each small group a Bible, and assign one of the following Scripture passages to each group:
- Matt. 5:44–45
- Matt. 21:18–22
- Eph. 6:18
- Phil. 4:6
- James 5:15–16

    Explain the assignment in your own words:
- In your small group, read aloud your passage and discuss what it teaches us about prayer. Let's have the reader be the person in each group with the shortest hair, and the reporter be the person with the longest hair. After you are done discussing the passage, your reporter will share with the whole group your small group's reflections.

    Allow enough time for the small groups to discuss their Scripture passage. Then invite the reporters to summarize their group's discussion.

5. Next, give each teen an index card and a pencil. Then say:
- The Bible describes the power of prayer. Let's use that power.

    On your card write one specific area of your life that could be improved by the power of prayer. For example, "patience with my younger brother," "support for a friend who is going through a rough time." Do not write your name on the index card. I will collect the cards and read them aloud during our closing prayer service. If you do not want your prayer read aloud, please indicate that on the card after writing your prayer.

6. When everyone is finished, collect the cards and save them for the closing prayer. Conclude the activity with words similar to these:

- God always answers our prayers, but doesn't always answer them with a miracle. The real joy of prayer is simply realizing that God, who created every living thing, wants an ongoing, intimate prayer relationship with you and with me. Prayers don't have to be requests. In fact, I would like to take a moment right now to pray a prayer of thanks to God. "Dear God, thank you so much for our time together and for the thoughts and prayers we've shared so far today. Continue to be with us as we journey through life. Amen."

(Based on Nappa, "The Power of Prayer," p. 62; and Nappa, *When God Seems Silent,* n.p.)

PRAY   Small-Group Activity (15 minutes)

This activity attempts to broaden the teens' ideas about where, why, and how one can pray.

Write the following on newsprint:

- P is for places.
- R is for reasons.
- A is for actions.
- Y is for your words.

Form small groups. Give each small group a piece of newsprint and a marker. Explain the following directions to the whole group:

- Divide your sheet of newsprint into four sections, one section for each of the above phrases relating to the word *pray.* Then, as a small group, brainstorm lists of the places where you pray, the reasons you pray, the kinds of actions that might be considered prayerful, and the types of words you use when you pray. Have a recorder write down your group's responses on the newsprint, and a reporter share them aloud when it is time. Let's have the recorder be the person in each group with the shortest middle name, and the reporter, the person with the longest middle name.

After everyone is finished, post the sheets of newsprint with masking tape, and invite the reporters to share their group's responses.

Convey the following conclusion in your own words:

- Prayer may be formal or informal. It may be done by yourself or with a group. The Scriptures may help us to pray and to reflect. Our personal experiences may also provide us with a starting point for our prayer. Some people find keeping a prayer journal helpful. Simply put, prayer is communication.

Anonymous Affirmations   (20 minutes)

This activity allows the retreatants to compliment one another anonymously.

Gather the group in a large circle and give each teen an index card and a pencil. Have the teens each write their name on their card. Then collect all the cards in a basket.

Pass the basket around the circle, and direct the teens to draw a name (not their own). Tell the teens to read the name, turn the card over, and write a compliment about the person whose name was drawn. Remind the teens to take the activity seriously and to write only positive comments.

Collect the cards and redistribute them, allowing the teens to write a compliment on another person's card. Continue in this fashion for several rounds.

After the final round, collect the cards again and return each card to the person whose name is on it. Give the young people a few minutes to read the anonymous compliments. If some people would like to share one of their written compliments, encourage them to do so.

Closing Prayer

Large-Group Activity (55–75 minutes)

The purpose of this exercise is to have the teens experience various forms of prayer: centering prayer, mantras, antiphonal prayer, petitional prayer, guided meditation, and journaling.

Ahead of time, photocopy handouts 4–C through 4–F back-to-back (double-sided) and assemble them into booklets by stapling them together. Handout 4–C is the cover. Each retreatant needs a booklet.

Gather the teens in a quiet spot for prayer, such as a church or chapel. It is important to change your location, if possible, to allow the teens to "shift gears."

The time in the prayer space will be divided up as follows: centering prayer (10–15 minutes), mantras (10–15 minutes), antiphonal prayer (5 minutes), petitional prayer (5 minutes), guided meditation (15–20 minutes), and journaling (10–15 minutes).

Centering Prayer

Introduce the activity with words similar to these:

• When you center yourself, you put yourself before God and become deeply aware of God's presence. In centering prayer you experience a real closeness to God—a God who is with you all the time, who wants to talk with you and spend time with you.

Centering prayer takes you inside yourself, to the center of your being, where God waits for you like a friend with a smile of welcome, a handshake of understanding, and a hug of love.

God wants to hear about your day. God says to you: "What has gone wrong in your day? What has gone right? What are you happy about? What are you sad about? What do you need and want? How do you feel about me?" (Adapted from Ready, *Praying* student booklet, p. 13)

The following recording is a centering prayer. Close your eyes, relax, and follow along with the tape. Try to truly concentrate on the words and images and not let your mind or heart be distracted.

Play the cassette segment "Sign of the Cross: A Guided Gesture Meditation on the Trinity," from *The Body at Prayer,* by Michael Sparough, music by Bobby Fisher (Cincinnati: Saint Anthony Messenger Press, 1987). Or substitute the following optional centering prayer.

Optional centering prayer. Read the following centering prayer slowly and reflectively. It works best if quiet instrumental music is played in the background.

- Close your eyes and relax. . . . Concentrate on your breathing. . . . With each breath in and out, slow down the pace. . . . Breathe in and out deeply, slowly, and fully. . . .

  Imagine in your mind a cross. . . . The cross is one of the most powerful symbols of our faith. . . . It can represent the Trinity, God.

  Now raise your right hand to your forehead as we begin a reflection on the sign of the cross. We begin in the name of God, the Creator. . . . Most of us say, "In the name of the Father," but some of us say, "Mother." What does this Father and Mother God provide for us? . . . God created us . . . knit us together in our mother's womb. . . . God gave us many talents and qualities . . . provided nature to sustain us and people to love us. . . .

  Now lower your right hand to your heart, saying, "In the name of the Son." . . . We pray to our Savior, Jesus Christ, who came to us in the form of a human being so that we could identify fully with him. . . . He knows how we feel. . . . He's experienced every emotion we have. . . . He knows sadness, disappointment, joy, and encouragement. . . .

  Now move your hand to your left shoulder and then your right shoulder, saying, "In the name of the Holy Spirit." Jesus promised us that we would never be alone. . . . So, on Pentecost, the gift of the Holy Spirit was given to us, . . . the Spirit of guidance, direction, support, and counsel. . . .

  Now put your hands in a prayer position with your palms together and fingers facing upward and say, "Amen." Yes, we believe in our God, in the Trinity. . . . This prayer to them is the prayer we begin most all other prayers with. . . .

  Now slowly open your eyes. . . . Together let us use our hands and our voice to pray the sign of the cross with new meaning and understanding. [Pray the sign of the cross as it is usually said.]

Mantras

Invite the teens to share aloud any advertising slogans or jingles they have heard. After several teens have spoken, ask the whole group:
- Why are these slogans effective?
- How do they make you feel?
- Are there any slogans or jingles that make you feel uncomfortable? Why?

  Continue by conveying the following information in your own words:
- Mantras are like jingles. They are repetitive, short, and easy to remember. They have a rhythm and beat, just like the pulse in your body. Just as your blood pulses through your body and gives you life, so, too, does prayer sustains and gives your spiritual body life.

Mantra means "breath prayer." You should be able to say a mantra with one breath. Mantras start by addressing God and usually have about eight syllables. They are meant to be short so that you can breathe them in and out. A mantra can be said at any time of the day or night—whenever you think of it or feel the need to say one. Some people say their mantra while they stand in line at a store. It helps them to be patient. Other people say their mantra while they wait for sleep to come. Some students say their mantra every time they enter or leave a classroom. A mantra is for the spare moments you have and for those times when you are under stress or feeling especially sad or especially happy. A mantra is a way of saying hello to God several times throughout the day.

You can change your mantra whenever you want to. You might say a mantra about anger for six weeks. Or you might say it for only one day. You might say a thank-you mantra to God for a week and then move on to a mantra about math. Your mantra is yours to say *when* you like and for as *long* as you like.

Before choosing a mantra, you need to get in touch with what you are most wishing for, with what you most want to say to God. Your mantra will help you talk with God and share your life with God. It can express sorrow, thanksgiving, praise, or love of God. Or your mantra can ask God for something important to you. Mantras are excellent ways of sharing your life with God. (Adapted from Ready, *Praying* student booklet, pp. 13–14)

Turn to page 1 of your prayer booklet for some examples of mantras.

Have the teens form pairs or groups of three. Give each pair or trio a copy of handout 4–B, "Mantra Worksheet," and a pencil. Have them create as many mantras as possible.

After several minutes, invite volunteers to share aloud the mantras their group wrote. Gently point out any that are not mantras.

Antiphonal Prayer

Divide the group into two sides, left and right. Give the whole group the following directions:
• Please turn to the antiphonal prayer, Psalm 16, on page 2 of your booklet. Antiphonal prayer is one of the oldest prayer forms in the church. It's unique alternating rhythm enables you to pray by both listening and speaking. It is important for your group (left or right) to speak together as one large body, so listen closely to those around you to make sure you are speaking in unison. Also, be an active listener. Your role is to listen and to speak. Finally, try to notice which line of the prayer speaks to you the most.

Have the whole group say the Psalm 16 prayer aloud. Repeat if necessary.

Petitional Prayer

Explain to the teens that examples of petitional prayers are the prayer requests an individual asks the whole community to offer to God. They may be more familiar with the term *prayers of the faithful,* which are heard at Mass. Tell the young people that their response to the prayers is, "Lord, hear our prayer." Read the petitions the teens wrote from the Power of Prayer activity, two or three at a time. After each set, say, "Let us pray to the Lord." Give them time to respond, "Lord, hear our prayer."

Guided Meditation

Begin the meditation with a progressive muscle relaxation exercise (see part C of the appendix for suggestions). If possible, play soft instrumental background music. Then continue with the following guided meditation. Pause for a few seconds at each ellipsis (. . .).

*   Imagine yourself in a big meadow on a bright sunny day. . . . The grass is very green, and all around you are fields of flowers. . . . The colors of the flowers range from golden yellow to crisp red. . . . There are pink and blue flowers of all shapes and sizes. . . . It is a very peaceful and beautiful place. . . . As you walk through the meadow, you see a small hill up ahead of you. . . . All of a sudden, you see someone coming over the hill. . . . Immediately you recognize him as Jesus. . . . You're feeling excited about meeting him, but a little nervous, too. . . .

    Behind Jesus are some other people, just a few at first. . . . They must be his disciples. You walk closer to them so that you can be with them and hear what they are saying. . . . As you get up next to them, you see behind them hundreds of people following Jesus and the disciples. . . . As far as you can see, there are men, women, and children following. . . . They want to be with Jesus, too, and hear him preach and heal the sick. . . . From what the disciples are saying, these people have been with Jesus all day, and now it is getting close to evening. . . .

    Jesus looks at the large crowd coming toward him and says to Philip, "Where can we buy enough bread for all these people to eat?" . . .

    Philip answers, "We would all have to work a month to buy enough bread for each person to have only a little piece." . . .

    Jesus' follower Andrew, Simon Peter's brother, says, "Here is a boy with five loaves of barley bread and two little fish, but that is not enough for so many people." . . .

    Jesus tells all the people to sit down. . . . There must be about five thousand here. . . .

    You see Jesus take the loaves of bread and the fish, thank God for them, and then distribute them to the people. . . . You help give out the bread and fish along with the other disciples. . . . As you do, you see the gratitude in the eyes of the people in the crowd. . . . You also see how tired they are, yet how filled with faith—faith that has brought them here to be with Jesus. . . . They truly believe in Jesus. . . .

    As you help the disciples clean up, you collect twelve baskets with the pieces left over from the five barley loaves and two little fish. . . . You have just witnessed a miracle. . . . Now Jesus approaches you and invites you to sit down and talk with him for a while. . . . You are in awe of this person and the miracle you just witnessed. . . .

Jesus asks, "How do you feel right now?" Share with Jesus your feelings and thoughts, especially about what you just witnessed. [Longer pause.]

Jesus continues by asking, "When have you truly felt God's presence?" Describe for Jesus a time when you knew God was with you or someone you know. [Longer pause.]

Jesus asks: "Tell me about a time when your prayer wasn't answered the way you thought it would be? How did you feel? What eventually happened?" [Longer pause.] Jesus responds: "I know it's disappointing when you don't get what you want. And it's hard to understand that God has a plan for you, but sometimes what you pray for is not in that plan. That doesn't mean God is distant or has forgotten you. God is very present, just in a different way." . . .

Jesus goes on and asks, "Can you tell me how God has changed your life in a significant way?" Spend time now sharing with Jesus about how God has changed your life. [Longer pause.] Now ask Jesus any questions you have, and listen to him respond to you. [Longer pause.]

Jesus says that it's time for him to go. He's very happy for having spent this time with you, and he hopes the two of you can get together again soon. . . .

The sun has almost set. . . . Everyone is gone, and Jesus leaves. . . . He walks back over the hill from which he came. . . . Now you no longer see him, but you feel very peaceful inside. . . . You sit down in the meadow and say a prayer for this day, this miracle, and for Jesus: "Jesus, thank you for all the miracles in my life, even the ones that are so small I may not recognize them as miracles. Thank you for supporting me during the tough times and rejoicing with me during the great times. Let me continue to realize that through prayer I can strengthen my friendship with you. Help me also to see that good friends help change one another for the better. Thank you for all the ways you have changed me. Continue to help me grow in my faith. Bless all the people I love and who love me, and may I always reach out to those around me. There I may touch hidden friends. Amen."

When you open your eyes, you will no longer be sitting in the meadow but back here in this room. When you are ready, slowly open your eyes and come back.

Journaling

In your own words, offer the teens the following explanation of journaling:

- Journaling is praying through writing. Just as we pray with words—either spoken aloud or silently to ourselves—we can also pray with written words. Journaling is like having a conversation with God. As you write down what you are thinking or feeling, God comes to you and can inspire you. After reading over a journal entry, many people not only feel better because they have expressed something and gotten it out of themselves, but also because they have gained new insights about themselves.

Have the teens turn to the back page of their booklet. In italics are samples of things they might write about. Explain that this is one way of journaling.

Direct the teens to think about a situation in their life that they would like to pray about. Have them use the journal outline as a guide. If possible, play soft instrumental music in the background.

Evaluation

Large Group (5 minutes)

After the journal writing, while still in the chapel or church, direct the teens to reflect in writing on the following questions. Invite them to answer aloud if they feel comfortable doing so.

- If you had only one word to describe today, what word would you pick?
- What is one new thing you learned today, or what is one thing you really liked? (It could be something we did or something someone said.)
- What do you feel God is challenging you to do as a result of this retreat?

Invite the teens to take their prayer booklet home with them and put it where they know they can find it if they need it in the future.

Jesus Changes Things

The object is to change the word at the top of each puzzle into the word at the bottom. You do this by changing one letter at a time, each time forming a new word. Jesus changed five loaves into tons. Can you?

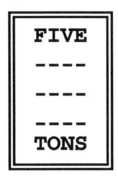

Now you are getting the hang of it!
Here are some more, all based on John 6:5–14:

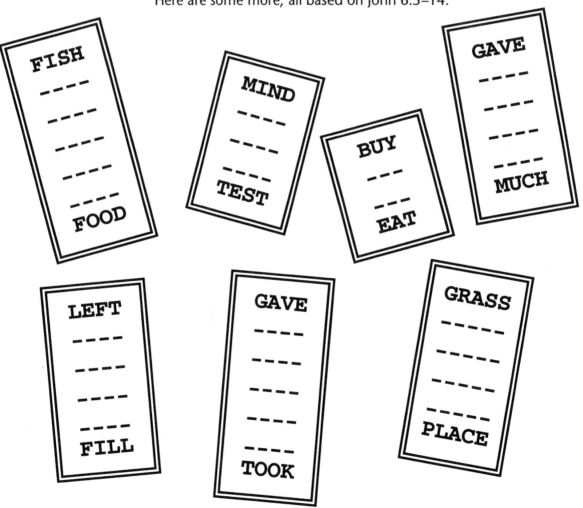

(Adapted from Tom Finley, *Good Clean Fun: Fifty More Nifty Games for Your Youth Group*, volume 2 [Grand Rapids, MI: Zondervan Publishing House, 1988], page 61)

Jesus Changes Things

The object is to change the word at the top of each puzzle into the word at the bottom. You do this by changing one letter at a time, each time forming a new word. Jesus changed five loaves into tons. Can you?

```
FIVE
FINE
FINS
TINS
TONS
```

Now you are getting the hang of it!
Here are some more, all based on John 6:5–14:

```
FISH          MIND              GAVE
FIST          MINT              GATE
MIST          TINT      BUY     MATE
MOST          TENT      BUT     MATH
MOOT          TEST      BAT     MACH
MOOD                    EAT     MUCH
FOOD

LEFT          GAVE              GRASS
LIFT          LAVE              GRADS
GIFT          LACE              GRADE
GILT          LACK              GRACE
GILL          LOCK              GLACE
FILL          LOOK              PLACE
              TOOK
```

(Adapted from Tom Finley, *Good Clean Fun: Fifty More Nifty Games for Your Youth Group,* volume 2 [Grand Rapids, MI: Zondervan Publishing House, 1988], page 61)

Prayer Quotes

"Any thoughts on prayer? Yeah. It's dumb." (Phlanax, from America On-line)

"Prayer is a very powerful thing. . . . It works for me." (Bridget2, from America Online)

"Prayer = brownie points with God." (Dave 911, from America Online)

"I believe in God, but I don't think God answers every prayer. One in 10,000 maybe." (Brenke, from America Online)

"So [you must] think clearly and control yourselves so you will be able to pray." (Peter, from the Bible, 1 Peter 4:7)

"I'm curious what makes people [pray]. It seems pointless to me." (Cuillin #2, from America Online)

"I think whether [prayer] works or not depends on the person praying. If you think it works, it probably will." (JENNYN3010, from America Online)

"Anyone who is having troubles should pray. . . . When a believing person prays, great things happen." (James, from the Bible, James 5:13–16)

"I don't think God really cares what God you pray to as long as you've said your prayers." (KathG, from America Online)

"God always answers, but the answer is not always yes." (Anonymous)

(Prayer quotes reprinted from Mike Nappa, *When God Seems Silent,* Group's Real Life Bible Curriculum [Loveland, CO: Group Publishing, 1995], no page)

Mantra Worksheet

Mantras are short prayers that start by addressing God. Most mantras have about eight syllables. They are meant to be short so that you can breathe them in and out.

Create a mantra for each of the following situations.
A. You've backed your parents' car into a tree.
B. You're on vacation at the beach and get up early one morning to witness a beautiful sunrise.
C. Your boyfriend or girlfriend is breaking up with you.
D. You're in your brother's wedding party, and you're about to walk down the aisle at the start of the ceremony.
E. You've just found out that your favorite uncle has a drug addiction.
F. Your best friend has just been caught cheating on a test.
G. You're sitting in a desk as the SAT exam is being passed out.
H. Create your own situation and mantra.

Handout 4–B: Permission to reproduce this handout for use in your program is granted.

91

Booklet Cover

Handout 4–C: Permission to reproduce this handout for use in your program is granted.

Mantras

Here are some examples of mantras:

◆ God, help me listen to others.

◆ God, thank you for your love.

◆ God, teach me to pray.

◆ God, help me know that you are near.

◆ God, help me stop getting angry.

◆ God, help me be a good friend.

◆ God, help me accept myself.

1

Handout 4–D: Permission to reproduce this handout for use in your program is granted.

93

Psalm 16

Left. Protect me, God,
        because I trust in you.
    I said to the LORD, "You are my Lord.
        Every good thing I have comes from you."

Right. As for the godly people in the world,
        they are the wonderful ones I enjoy.
    But those who turn to idols
        will have much pain.

Left. I will not offer blood to those idols
        or even speak their names.
    No, the LORD is all I need.
        He takes care of me.

Right. My share in life has been pleasant;
        my part has been beautiful.
    I praise the LORD because he advises me.
        Even at night, I feel his leading.

Left. I keep the LORD before me always.
    Because he is close by my side,
    I will not be hurt.

Right. So I rejoice and am glad.
    Even my body has hope,
because you will not leave me in the grave.

Left. You will not let your holy one rot.
    You will teach me how to live a holy life.

All. Being with you will fill me with joy;
    at your right hand I will find pleasure forever.

(Youth Bible, New Century Version
[Dallas: Word Publishing, 1991], pages 489–490)

2

Journaling

Today's Date: _____

I feel:
(unsure, confident, scared, excited)

Prayer:
(Please give me the courage to strive high . . . to try my hardest in all I do to be a success. Be with me also when I fail, so I can have the reassurance of success another time.)

Personal reflection:
(Today I found out that I'm not doing as well as I thought I was doing in . . .)

Today I will:
(spend an extra ten minutes improving . . .)

3

Handout 4–F: Permission to reproduce this handout for use in your program is granted.

95

Retreat 5

Self-Esteem

Theme   This retreat helps young people to see themselves as unique individuals and to feel good about who God made them to be.

Bible Basis   *1 Sam. 16:1,6–7.* Through Samuel we are reminded to go beyond exterior characteristics and look for the inner qualities that make a person special.

Objectives   The retreatants will do the following:
- define the word *self-esteem*
- assess and appreciate their unique internal and external qualities
- examine the influence of the media on their self-image
- develop skills for building self-esteem
- reaffirm the belief that God loves each person unconditionally

Retreat at a Glance

The following chart offers a brief overview of the retreat activities, time frames, and materials needed. For more detailed information about any of the activities, refer to the directions given in the Retreat in Detail section.

ACTIVITY	TIME FRAME	SUPPLIES
Welcome and Introduction	10–15 minutes	poster with standards
Icebreakers	15–30 minutes	depends on selection
Opening Prayer	5 minutes	Bible
I'm This, Not That	10 minutes	marker, two signs
Who Would You Choose?	20–25 minutes	poster board, pictures of people, glue or tape, paper, pencils
Perfect in Every Way	15 minutes	poster board, picture of presidents, eggs, candy, colored paper
Break	10 minutes	
Scripture Sculpting	15–20 minutes	handout 5–A
Self-Esteem Scramble	5–10 minutes	uninflated balloons, small slips of paper, scissors, pencil or pen
Top That	10 minutes	old hat
Overcoming Obstacles	20–30 minutes	
Lunch	45 minutes	
Icebreakers	15 minutes	depends on selection
Past Achievements	15 minutes	newsprint, marker
Positive Self-Talk	20–30 minutes	newsprint, marker, handout 5–B
Famous People and Famous Me	30–35 minutes	newsprint, marker, index cards, pencils, handout 5–C
Pat on the Back	15–20 minutes	newsprint, markers, poster board, safety pins or masking tape
Closing Guided Meditation	20–30 minutes	instrumental music, tape or CD player
Evaluation	5 minutes	pencils, paper

Retreat in Detail

Welcome and Introduction

(10–15 minutes)

Icebreakers

(15–30 minutes)

Choose from among the icebreakers offered in part A of the appendix of this book, or use games of your own.

Opening Prayer

(5 minutes)

Begin the prayer by reading 1 Sam. 16:1,6–7—the account of God's choice of David as king of the Israelites. Finish by sharing the following prayer in your own words:

• Dear God, like Samuel, we sometimes make decisions based on what people look like. We tend to believe that good-looking people are the chosen people. God reminded Samuel, and God reminds us, that there is more to a person than what is on the surface. God makes decisions based on the strengths and gifts that are inside of people.

God, before we make decisions based on external qualities, remind us to take the time to get to know people and see their internal qualities. Thank you for the gift of our own self-esteem. May we always appreciate our self-esteem and the self-esteem of others. Amen.

I'm This, Not That

Large-Group Activity (10 minutes)

The purpose of this activity is for the teens to identify some of their personal characteristics.

Make two signs: one labeled "Side A," and the other, "Side B." Post the signs on opposite sides of the room.

Give the teens these directions, stated in your own words:

• I will read a series of two opposing characteristics, for example, "Are you more like a rabbit or a turtle?" If you are more like a rabbit, move to side A. If you are more like a turtle, move to side B.

Read aloud the following characteristics, pausing after each set to allow the young people to make a decision and move to the appropriate side of the room. If you wish, invite volunteers to explain their choice.

Side A		*Side B*
• Mercedes-Benz	or	Ford Escort
• winter	or	summer
• artist	or	accountant
• listener	or	talker
• spender	or	saver
• leader	or	follower
• doer	or	thinker
• player	or	spectator
• easygoing	or	hyperactive

At the end of the activity, lead a discussion with the whole group based on the following questions (see the introduction for alternative ways of debriefing this and other retreat activities):

• What can an exercise like this teach us?

• Why is it important to know our personal characteristics?

Offer a conclusion like this to the activity:
- Self-esteem consists of seeing and appreciating the various characteristics and talents we possess and have developed. During our retreat together, we hope to explore self-esteem further.

Who Would You Choose?

Small-Group Activity (20–25 minutes)

In this activity the teens realize that even though it's easier to judge people by how they look, we need to see beyond just the physical.

Before the retreat, glue or tape pictures of people of all races, genders, and ages on a piece of poster board. Number each picture. Form small groups and give each group a sheet of paper and a pencil. Introduce the activity by saying something like this:
- I am going to ask you a series of questions, and you are to answer them by choosing pictures of people on the poster. After each question, I will pause so your group can discuss it and decide on the people whom you would choose. One person in each group needs to be the recorder, who writes down the number or numbers of the picture(s) the group chooses for each question. The group also needs a reporter, who will share the answers during the discussion period. Let's have the person in each group with the longest last name be the recorder, and the person with the shortest last name be the reporter.

Make sure that all groups can see the poster. (If you have a large group, you may want to make several identical posters, one for each group.) Pose the following questions to the teens, pausing after each one so that the groups can discuss and write down their answers:
- Which five people would you want to travel with for one year? Why?
- Is there any one person you would not want anything to do with? Why?
- Who, if anyone, would you be willing to marry? Why or why not?
- Who, if anyone, would you choose to be your best friend? Why or why not?
- If only five of the people photographed and yourself were allowed to live, and everyone else would be executed, which five would stay with you? Why?
- What traits, other than how people look, would you prefer to use to answer these questions?

(Adapted from Yaconelli and Koenigsaecker, *Get 'Em Talking*, p. 93)

Perfect in Every Way

Large-Group Activity (15 minutes)

Before the retreat, gather the following items: four eggs, pictures of four different presidents, four different types of candy, and four sheets of paper, each of a different color.

Place all these items on a table. Direct the group to examine the items carefully. After the teens have studied the items, ask the whole group these questions:
- Which of the presidents pictured here was the closest to being perfect? Why?
- Which one of the eggs is the most perfect egg? Why?
- Which piece of paper is the most perfect color? Why?
- Which kind of candy is the most perfect? Why?

The teens will likely have a range of opinions. They may use different criteria for selecting the "best" item in each group. Explain that any one of these items could be considered best, and no one example from these groups is absolutely perfect.

Lead a large-group discussion of the following questions:
- How many perfect people have you met in your lifetime?
- If you haven't met a perfect person, what are your chances for meeting one?
- Do you think it is possible to be perfect? What would that be like?

Offer the following thoughts in your own words:
- Perfectionism may keep us from feeling good about ourselves. We need to accept ourselves for who we are and not expect our bodies to be perfect, because physical characteristics are often out of our control. For example, if it really bothers you that you are too tall, there's not much you can do to become shorter, but you could stop telling yourself it is terrible to be so tall and try focusing on your positive qualities instead.

Guide the young people in a discussion of what physical aspects they think they can change and what aspects they think they will have to accept. For example:
- If you dislike your hair, you could get a different style.
- If you think you are too fat or too thin, you could see the school nurse or your family physician for advice on diet.
- If you think your feet are too big, you will probably have to learn to live with them the way they are.
- If you think you are uncoordinated, you could take dance or karate lessons.

Break (10 minutes)

Scripture Sculpting

Small-Group Activity (15–20 minutes)
This activity helps the teens appreciate that God loves us not only for our external qualities but also for our internal ones.

1. Divide the large group into six small groups. Give each group a copy of handout 5–A, "Scripture Sculpting." Assign one of the readings on the handout to each group.

In your own words, explain who Samuel was and what his role was, in case some of the teens do not know:
- After the American Revolution in the 1770s, the thirteen states were almost like independent countries. Each had its own laws, and they constantly bickered. Only after the country had a new constitution and a strong president, George Washington, did the states unite.

  The Israelites in Samuel's time lived in a similar situation. They didn't have any central government or regular army. For about a hundred years, the tribes had come together only during crises.

  But the Israelites lived in constant fear of the Philistines. This warlike nation with superior iron weapons controlled the fertile plains along the Mediterranean Sea and wanted to add to its territory. So the Philistines wanted to conquer the Israelites and take their land.

To survive, the independent tribes had to unite and stop the invaders. They needed a leader to unite them to stand up to the threat. That leader would be Samuel.

As it turned out, Samuel changed Israel's history. He stopped the Philistines from advancing, and, even more important, he appointed Israel's first two kings: King Saul and King David. (Youth Bible, pp. 244–245)

In the Scripture passage on the handout, Samuel first assumes Eliab is to be chosen as king because he is so good looking. But God wanted David to be king.

2. Explain the activity this way:
• Each small group has a piece of a Scripture passage from the Book of Samuel. Your group is to create a mime to illustrate your short section. The goal is for each group to follow the previous group's mime in sequence so that the story flows smoothly. I will read the Scripture passage slowly, and each of you are to do your mime as I am reading your section aloud. Once we have practiced, we will mime the passage in silence.

At first the teens will most likely laugh. Allow that to happen until they are comfortable with the exercise. If the teens are still restless, explain that the goal is to make this a prayer using our body, not our mouth.

Give the teens enough time to practice in their small group and then with verbal narration. Perform the Scripture passage in silence.

3. Lead a discussion with the whole group based on the following questions:
• How did you feel while performing the mime?
• How is performing the mime like expressing your self-esteem?
• What, if anything, made performing the mime in silence different from performing it with my verbal narration?
• What does this particular passage say to us about God? ourselves? others?

Self-Esteem Scramble

Small-Group Activity (5–10 minutes)

The purpose of this activity is to give the teens this definition of self-esteem to think about: Self-esteem is loving yourself the way God loves you.

Ahead of time, write or type the definition of self-esteem on a sheet of paper. Make a copy of the definition for each small group. Cut each copy of the definition into nine clues, one word per piece of paper. Put each set of clues in an uninflated balloon. Prepare a balloon for each small group.

1. Distribute an uninflated balloon containing the clues to each small group. Explain the following procedure:
• Each small group blows up its balloon and ties it. One person in the group volunteers to sit on the balloon until it breaks, releasing the nine clues. The first team to break the balloon and unscramble the mystery sentence wins.

2. After all have pieced together the definition, lead a large-group discussion of these questions:
- How do we know God loves us?
- How do we know God accepts us for who we are?

3. Continue with a presentation like the following:
- Sometimes we believe that our self-esteem comes from what society tells us is the ideal person. We judge people on the basis of intelligence, beauty, performance, and economic and social status. The media certainly hype this ideal—so much so that if we fall short in any of these criteria, we may view ourselves as unworthy or unimportant. We compare ourselves to others, and other people compare themselves to us. Instead of focusing on *society's* definition of self-worth, we need to remind ourselves that self-esteem is loving ourselves the way God loves us. We are made in the image and likeness of God. We are very special people. We are not perfect; no one is. It's not always easy to feel lovable, especially with all the pressure out there to be perfect.

  Self-esteem can also be defined as the mental picture we have of ourselves. If we could block out the influences of both the media and negative people around us, it would be easier to live with a positive self-image. Unfortunately we are bombarded by negative messages, so we have to work extra hard at believing in ourselves and ignoring others who want to bring us down. Many people in history believed in themselves rather than in what others said about them. For example:
  - An expert once said that Vince Lombardi (famous coach of the Green Bay Packers) possessed minimal football knowledge and lacked motivation.
  - Louisa May Alcott, the author of *Little Women,* was encouraged by her family to find work as a servant or seamstress.
  - Beethoven handled the violin awkwardly and preferred playing his own compositions instead of improving his technique. His teacher called him hopeless as a composer.
  - Walt Disney was fired by a newspaper editor for lack of ideas. He also went bankrupt several times before he built Disneyland.
  - Albert Einstein did not speak until he was four years old and didn't read until he was seven. His teacher described him as "mentally slow, unsociable and adrift forever in his foolish dreams." He was expelled and was refused admittance to the Zurich Polytechnic School.
  - Louis Pasteur was only a mediocre pupil in undergraduate studies and ranked fifteenth out of twenty-two in chemistry.
  - The sculptor Rodin's father once said that he had an idiot for a son. Described as the worst pupil in the school, Rodin failed three times to secure admittance to the school of art. His uncle called him uneducable.
  - Henry Ford failed and went broke five times before he finally succeeded.

○ Babe Ruth, considered by sports historians to be the greatest
athlete of all time, and famous for setting the home run record,
also holds the record for strikeouts.

(Adapted from Canfield and Hansen,
Chicken Soup for the Soul, pp. 228–230)

Now would be an appropriate time to share a personal story about
the development of your own self-esteem and how God has helped you.

4. You may want to conclude by saying something like this:

• Some people say, "Well, if I act really confident, others will think
I'm conceited," or "It's not really true that I have this good quality."
Whether it is true or not, what *you* believe about yourself is important. Others help reveal the gift of who you are, the gift God created
you to be. However, it still comes down to how much you believe you
are loved by God and to the mental picture you have of yourself. I
hope that the people who surround you help to build up your self-
esteem.

Top That — Large-Group Activity (10 minutes)

In this activity the teens distinguish between pride and arrogance with
regard to self-esteem.

Have everyone sit in a circle and introduce the activity this way:

• You've all seen this kind of thing happen. People start bragging
about how smart they are or how smart their dog is or how fast their
car is. Suddenly another person interrupts saying, "I can top that!"
and starts bragging about something else.

Put on an old hat and say:

• This is a bragger's hat. I'm going to begin by bragging about something true or untrue about myself. Then I'll toss the hat to someone
else. That person is to put on the hat and "top" my story. Then that
person will toss the hat to another person. We will continue until
several people have had a chance to top one another.

Begin the activity. Play until about five or six teens have had the
hat. Then ask the whole group:

• What did you learn about yourself during this activity?

• How do you feel when people try to top one another in real-life
conversations?

• Will this experience change the way you will respond to bragging
competitions in the future? How?

• What's the difference between bragging and self-esteem? between
arrogance and self-esteem?

Conclude by conveying these ideas in your own words:

• Trying to top what our friends do and say may be fun in a situation
like this one. But when it happens in real life, everybody usually goes
away feeling put down or unappreciated. This kind of arrogant behavior can lead to some serious consequences in our relationships.

(Adapted from Younger, *Overcoming Insecurities*, pp. 23–24)

Overcoming Obstacles — Small-Group Activity (20–30 minutes)

This activity makes the young people aware that all people, even
famous people, must face and try to overcome obstacles.

Form small groups. Have each small group think of a famous person, living or dead, who overcame either a physical obstacle or a prejudice. Explain to the small groups that they are to create a skit with this person in it without mentioning the person's name. The other small groups will try to guess which famous person each small group is portraying.

After the small groups have all performed their role-plays and all famous persons have been identified, lead a discussion of these questions with the whole group:
- What helped these famous people overcome their disability or prejudice?
- Who helped these people succeed?
- How do you think these people would define self-esteem?

Lunch (45 minutes)

Icebreakers (15 minutes)
Choose from among the icebreakers offered in part A of the appendix of this book, or use games of your own.

Past Achievements Large-Group Activity (15 minutes)
This activity and the ones that follow it give the teens some techniques to use to rebuild their self-esteem when it is damaged.

Introduce the activity by saying something like this:
- It would be wonderful if we could go through life always feeling great about ourselves. However, we know that is not reality. We don't feel good about ourselves every day. Sometimes we fail a test or get yelled at for forgetting to do something. Sometimes we just have a bad hair day. It's at those times that we need to rebuild our self-esteem. Let's go over some ways of rebuilding self-esteem, and then you can share things you have done to repair your self-esteem.

On newsprint write, "Past Achievements," and convey the following information in your own words:
- Sometimes when we are having a bad day, we begin to think that every day will continue to be lousy. That's when we have to look back and remember the high points in our life, the days when we felt really great about ourselves. When I call out the following items, I want you to raise your hand if any of them pertain to you.
  ○ Has anyone here ever been on a winning team?
  ○ How about moving—has anyone here ever survived a move?
  ○ Who did not make it through their first scary day of kindergarten?
  ○ Have any of you ever finished a project or paper you thought you could never do?
  ○ Has anyone ever won an award for something—sports? school accomplishments? service? scouts? attendance? a hobby?
  ○ Has anyone ever scored a winning point? caught a winning pass? hit a winning run?
  ○ Has anyone ever passed a difficult test?
  ○ Has anyone ever made it through a day while not feeling well?
  ○ Has anyone delivered newspapers in the rain?
  ○ Has anyone ever been hired for a job?

○ Has anyone passed a driver's test?

○ Has anyone ever recovered from an injury such as a broken arm or leg?

○ Has anyone ever recovered from an operation?

We have all had achievements in our life. We have all had success of one kind or another. We need to remember this when we're down on ourselves. I want you to think of a time when you felt proud of yourself. It could have been when you were in second grade or yesterday. The time doesn't matter.

Direct everyone to gather with their small group and take turns sharing about their achievements.

Conclude the activity by posing these questions to the whole group:

• What did you learn in your small group?

• How might looking back at our achievements help us in the future?

(Adapted from Rubly-Burggraff, *Look Who's Drivin' the Bus,* unit 1, session 3, pp. 5–6)

Positive Self-Talk

Small-Group Role-Plays (20–30 minutes)

In this activity the teens practice giving themselves positive affirmations to diminish the effects of destructive comments and messages they receive from other people, society, and the media.

Write "Positive Self-Talk" on a sheet of newsprint. Then say:

• Another way to rebuild our self-esteem is to practice giving ourselves positive messages. We tend to listen more to negative ideas and comments than to positive ones.

Photocopy handout 5–B, "Positive Self-Talk Situations." Give each small group a copy. Go over the directions on the handout with them, and assign a role-play situation to each small group.

Give the groups 5 minutes or so to practice their role-play. Then invite the groups to take turns performing their role-play.

Conclude the activity by leading a whole-group discussion of the following questions:

• Was it easy or difficult to come up with negative messages? with positive messages? Why?

• In real life why don't we always let the positive statements win?

• Is it always necessary to have a longer list of positive messages than negative messages in order to do the right thing, or is having one or two really persuasive positive statements enough? Why?

• What can a person do to help the positive messages win?

• How is positive self-talk connected to self-esteem?

Famous People and Famous Me

Small-Group Activity (30–35 minutes)

The purpose of this activity is for the teens to identify the qualities that make them unique.

1. On a sheet of newsprint write, "Affirming Ourselves." Introduce the exercise in your own words:

• This is like the previous exercise in which we gave ourselves positive messages. In this activity we get to identify the qualities we appreciate about ourselves and proclaim them proudly to others.

Give each small group a 3-by-5-inch index card and a pencil. Direct each group to think of someone famous, living or dead. Have them write that person's name across the top of the index card and then add three sentences that person might use to describe himself or herself.

2. Collect the cards. Read the sentences aloud, and have the teens guess who is being described.

Next, ask the whole group:
- How do people become known for certain abilities or characteristics?
- What makes someone famous?

3. This time give each teen a 3-by-5-inch index card and a copy of handout 5–C, "Internal and External Qualities."

On newsprint, list the following items:
- first name
- two external qualities
- three internal qualities
- two interests, hobbies, or talents
- Thank you, God, for giving me _____; for making me _____.

Give the whole group the following directions, stated in your own words:
- On the newsprint is an outline for describing yourself. On your handout are some suggested internal and external qualities. You may use qualities from the handout or others you think of on your own. Write on your index card the qualities that best describe you. Just like last time, I will collect the cards, read the qualities and talents aloud, and invite the whole group to try to guess whom I am talking about. Please complete this exercise quietly, and do not let anyone else see what you are writing. When you have completed your index card, please bring it up to me.

Some teens may not feel comfortable with this activity, especially with having their qualities read aloud in step 4. If they resist, urge them to complete the exercise and then write on the top of their card, "Do not read aloud."

4. After collecting all the index cards, gather the teens in one large circle. Read the index cards aloud, pausing after each one so that the whole group can try to guess the identity of the person. Applaud when the person's identity is guessed correctly.

5. Lead a discussion with the whole group based on the following questions:
- What was easy about this exercise? What was difficult?
- How do our internal and external qualities contribute to our self-esteem? take away from our self-esteem?

Invite the teens to take their index card home with them.

Pat on the Back Affirmation (15–20 minutes)

In this activity the young people affirm one another through touch and words.

On the same sheet of newsprint used in the previous activity, under "Affirming Ourselves," write, "Accepting Affirmation from Others." Say something like this:
- Another way to rebuild our self-esteem is to see ourselves through the eyes of other people and to accept compliments and praise from them.

Pin or tape a piece of poster board on the back of each teen. Give each person a marker. Explain these instructions in your own words:
- Mingle around the room, writing a compliment on the back of as many people as time allows. After writing your compliment, give that person a gentle pat on the back. You may sign your name if you choose, or you may remain anonymous.

After about 15 minutes, have the teens help one another remove their poster board. Give them time to read over their list of compliments.

Closing Guided Meditation

(20–30 minutes)

Begin the meditation with a progressive muscle relaxation exercise (see part C of the appendix for suggestions). If possible, play soft instrumental background music. Then continue with the following guided meditation. Pause for a few seconds at each ellipsis (. . .).
- Self-esteem is something we work on every day of our life. Our self-esteem is a gift from God and consists of how we view both our internal and our external qualities. It would be great if we always felt wonderful about ourselves. Unfortunately, however, we all have days when we have to rebuild our self-esteem due to various circumstances. Jesus encountered many people who felt badly about themselves. Just as he lifted up these people, so, too, can he lift us up.

    Imagine yourself living during the time of Jesus. . . . You're on the road to Jerusalem. The air is very still, and everything is dry. . . . It is late afternoon, and the sky is turning mellow colors of pink and purple as the sun slowly sets. . . . Up ahead—off the side of the road—you suddenly see a group of ten men. . . . They are away from the road because they are not allowed to be with the rest of the people. . . . They have leprosy and are therefore isolated from others so as not to spread the dreaded disease. . . . At the same time, you see Jesus coming toward you on the road. . . . As Jesus passes the men, all ten of them shout together: "Jesus, Master! Have mercy on us!" . . . When Jesus sees them, he says, "Go and show yourselves to the priests." . . . As the ten men go, you notice that they no longer appear to have leprosy. . . .

    Now Jesus is right next to you and invites you to sit down. . . . Jesus says, "How are you feeling right now? . . . Spend time sharing with Jesus. [Longer pause.] Jesus continues, "What's one physical characteristic you like about yourself and why?" [Longer pause.] Jesus then asks: "What's one inner quality you are really proud of about yourself?" [Longer pause.] "What's one quality you'd like me to help you develop more of?" [Longer pause.]

    As you finish talking to Jesus, you are suddenly interrupted by one of the ten men whom Jesus just healed of leprosy. . . . He came back to thank Jesus. . . . Jesus responds: "Weren't ten men healed? Where are the other nine?" . . . The man says he doesn't know. . . . Jesus says: "Go on your way. You were healed because you believed." . . . The man turns and leaves. . . . You can see the joy and gratitude in his face. . . .

Jesus then continues: "Tell me about a time when you were really grateful that God made you the person you are." [Longer pause.]

Jesus asks you to tell him about one of your greatest possessions. . . . Think of something you truly treasure. Tell Jesus what it is and why it is so important to you. [Longer pause.] Now Jesus shares with you one of his greatest possessions. . . . He opens up his wallet, and inside is a picture of you. . . . Share with Jesus how this makes you feel. [Longer pause.]

Jesus says that he must go now but has enjoyed his time with you. . . . Before he goes he wants to know if you would like to talk with him about anything else. . . . Spend these last few minutes talking with Jesus or sitting quietly with him. [Longer pause.]

Jesus stands and begins to walk down the road. . . . You can no longer see him, but you feel his presence very close to you. . . . You're motivated to say a prayer: "Jesus, thank you for sharing this time with me and for making me feel so good about myself. Help me always remember to be like the healed man who was so grateful that he returned and thanked you. Let me always remember my good qualities, and help me rebuild my self-esteem when I feel low and unhappy with myself. Amen."

When you open your eyes, you will no longer be on the road but back here in this room. When you are ready, slowly open your eyes and come back.

Evaluation

Large Group (5 minutes)

After the guided meditation, direct the teens to reflect in writing on the following questions. Invite them to answer aloud if they feel comfortable doing so.

- If you had only one word to describe today, what word would you pick?
- What is one new thing you learned from this retreat, or what is one thing you really liked? (It could be something you did or something someone said.)
- What do you feel God is challenging you to do as a result of this retreat?

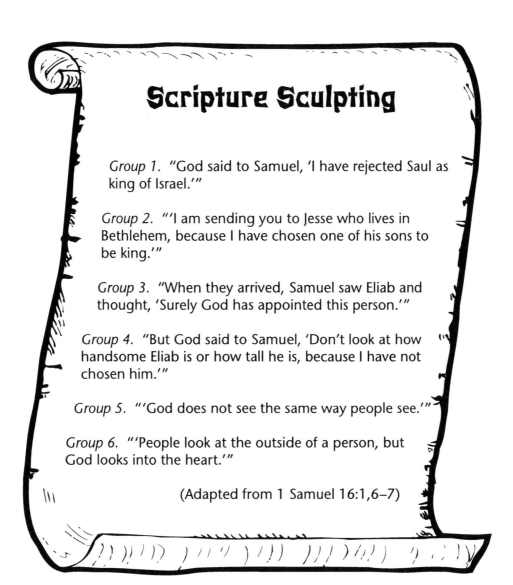

Scripture Sculpting

Group 1. "God said to Samuel, 'I have rejected Saul as king of Israel.'"

Group 2. "'I am sending you to Jesse who lives in Bethlehem, because I have chosen one of his sons to be king.'"

Group 3. "When they arrived, Samuel saw Eliab and thought, 'Surely God has appointed this person.'"

Group 4. "But God said to Samuel, 'Don't look at how handsome Eliab is or how tall he is, because I have not chosen him.'"

Group 5. "'God does not see the same way people see.'"

Group 6. "'People look at the outside of a person, but God looks into the heart.'"

(Adapted from 1 Samuel 16:1,6–7)

Handout 5–A: Permission to reproduce this handout for use in your program is granted.

109

Positive Self-Talk Situations

The purpose of role-playing the following situations is to come up with positive self-talk messages that a person might give herself or himself when experiencing low self-esteem.

In each of the following situations, one person in the small group plays the "devil," or negative thoughts; another person plays the "angel," or positive thoughts; and another person plays the person who's thinking out loud.

The devil and the angel act like shadows to the person in the middle. Each time the person wonders out loud about how to deal with the situation and how it might affect him or her, the angel expresses affirming thoughts about the person, and the devil expresses put-downs or negative thoughts about the person.

Try to end your role-play with the angel, or positive thoughts, winning.

Situation 1. You have confided in a good friend that you are gay. Your friend is shocked by this and is not sure whether to remain friends with you.

Situation 2. Your father is an alcoholic who has never said anything nice to you or about you. You recently received a scholarship to an Ivy League school and are not sure if you should take it. Your dad doesn't think you're capable of succeeding at an Ivy League school.

Situation 3. You and your best friend both like the same guy (or girl). You've just discovered that the guy (girl) you like has asked your friend out. You're hurt and disappointed and are beginning to feel that you're not good looking enough or that you'll never find a boyfriend (girlfriend).

Situation 4. You and your friend are competing to be on the same sports team. You just learned that your friend made the team but you did not. You're angry, hurt, and feeling down on yourself.

Situation 5. You are the star player on the sports team but got injured recently and are out for the season. You're worried if this will affect your scholarship potential.

Situation 6. Your parents have just informed you that they are divorcing. You knew they were having problems, but you always thought they would work it out. You're wondering if you had anything to do with this.

Situation 7. You've always been good in math and had planned on a career as an engineer, but this year you are failing geometry. It seems no matter what you do you can't pass. It's really getting you down.

Internal and External Qualities

Internal Qualities

aggressive	ambitious	artistic	athletic
blunt	careless	creative	cheerful
courageous	compassionate	demanding	determined
enthusiastic	energetic	faithful	forceful
forgiving	friendly	funny	generous
gentle	attentive	handy	unforgiving
hopeful	impatient	jealous	just
joyful	kind	loving	loyal
musical	neat	negative	organized
overpowering	patient	persevering	picky
positive	quiet	responsible	selfish
shy	trustworthy	understanding	

others *(add your own)*:

External Qualities

name	hair color	hairstyle	height
eye color	skin tone	shoe size	weight
figure or build	clothes		

others *(add your own)*:

Handout 5–C: Permission to reproduce this handout for use in your program is granted.

111

Retreat 6

Sexuality

Theme   This retreat invites teens to see their sexuality as a gift from God and to learn how to appropriately share that gift with others.

Bible Basis   *Gen. 1:26–31.* In Genesis, God reminds us that we have been created male and female in the image of God. As God's special creations, we are challenged to share the gift of our sexuality responsibly.

Objectives   The retreatants will do the following:
- affirm their own unique gift of maleness or femaleness
- identify the influence of outside forces on their understanding of sexuality
- define intimacy and see it as a value in relationships
- examine the Scriptures to help them understand sexuality as a gift from God
- review techniques for resisting sexual pressure

Retreat at a Glance

The following chart offers a brief overview of the retreat activities, time frames, and materials needed. For more detailed information about any of the activities, refer to the directions given in the Retreat in Detail section.

ACTIVITY	TIME FRAME	SUPPLIES
Welcome and Introduction	10–15 minutes	poster with standards
Icebreakers	15–30 minutes	depends on selection
Opening Prayer	5 minutes	Bible
Yes, No, Maybe	10–15 minutes	
Male and Female— What's the Difference?	20 minutes	poster board, markers, newsprint, Jungian chart
Yin Yang	15–20 minutes	handout 6–A, pencils
Break	10 minutes	
Defining Sexuality	15 minutes	poster board, markers, index cards, pencils
Attitudes	10 minutes	newsprint, markers
Intimate Couples	30 minutes	poster board, markers, TV guides, Bible
Lunch	45 minutes	
Icebreakers	15 minutes	depends on selection
Perfect Mate	15 minutes	handout 6–B, pencils
The Scriptures and Sexuality	15 minutes	Bibles, paper, pencils
Fact or Feeling?	10–15 minutes	Bible
Honey, If You Love Me	10 minutes	
Sex Stress Strategies	20–30 minutes	poster board or newsprint, markers
Twenty Ways to Say "I Love You"	10 minutes	newsprint, markers
Many Thanks	15–20 minutes	
Closing Guided Meditation	20–30 minutes	instrumental music, tape or CD player
Evaluation	5 minutes	pencils, paper

Retreat in Detail

Welcome and Introduction

(10–15 minutes)

Icebreakers

(15–30 minutes)

Choose from among the icebreakers offered in part A of the appendix of this book, or use games of your own.

Opening Prayer

(5 minutes)

Begin the prayer by reading the following Scripture passage:

- Then God said: "Let us make human beings in our image and likeness. And let them rule over the fish in the sea and the birds in the sky, over the tame animals, over all the earth, and over all the small crawling animals on the earth." So God created human beings in God's image. In the divine image God created them. God created them male and female. God blessed them and said, "Have many children and grow in number. . . ." And it happened. God looked at everything God had made, and it was very good. (Adapted from Gen. 1:26–31)

  Finish with a prayer similar to the following:

- Dear God, we thank you for the gift of our life. We praise you as our Creator. As males and females, you have created each of us in your image. May we gain a greater understanding of the wonderful and powerful gift of sexuality. Give us the strength, O God, to make good choices and to develop right attitudes in regard to love and sex. When we are tempted, be our guide. May we see the gift of sexuality as sacred and as reserved for the real love of marriage. May we not be swayed by today's casual attitudes toward sex. Amen.

Yes, No, Maybe

Large-Group Activity (10–15 minutes)

This activity challenges the retreatants to think about and articulate what they believe about sex, sexuality, and gender issues. The responses will help you, the retreat director, understand where the teens are coming from regarding sex and sexuality. At the end of the retreat, you could ask some of these questions again to see if the teens' opinions have changed.

Have the students sit in chairs in a circle, and give them these directions in your own words:

- I am going to read a series of statements one at a time. If you agree with the statement, stand up in front of your chair. If you disagree with it, sit on the floor in front of your chair. If you are not sure, remain seated in your chair.

  After reading each statement, direct the teens to make their choice. Invite volunteers to say why they agree or disagree with the statement or why they are unsure about it. Do not attempt to correct the retreatants' perspectives. This may be difficult to do, but keep in mind that your role is one of facilitator, not teacher. Just keep challenging the young people to defend their position. Use follow-up questions such as these:

- How have you come to believe _____?

- What would make you change your mind?
- What makes it so hard to believe _____?
  Here are the statements:
- God hates sex.
- My parents are embarrassed about sex.
- Television affects people's sexual values.
- There are no absolute sexual values. I determine what is right for me.
- Virginity is a desirable trait.
- Living together is a good alternative to marriage.
- Jesus struggled with his sexuality.
- You know you are in love when you "feel" you are.
- A person can fall in love only once.
- Love can conquer all.
- Love is blind.
- True love lasts forever.
- Sex is permissible if the two people are truly in love.
- Love at first sight is real.
- Men who stay at home while their wives go to work are lazy.
- Men make good secretaries and nurses.
- Women should make the decisions in the family.
- Only women can take care of the household and cook the meals.
- If my parents don't approve of the person I am dating, I should stop seeing him or her.
- Couples should share expenses on a date.
- "Fooling around" is okay as long as the couple does not go all the way.

Male and Female— What's the Difference?

Small-Group Activity (20 minutes)

This activity asks the teens to identify the unique gifts that men and women have, and it introduces the concept of complementarity between the sexes.

Before the retreat, make a poster listing Carl Jung's determination of masculine and feminine traits. Use the following chart as a model:

Feminine and Masculine Traits According to Jung

Feminine Traits	*Masculine Traits*
Nurturance	Responsibility
Receptivity	Assertiveness
Passivity	Activity
Subjectivity	Objectivity
Emotionality	Rationality
Intuition	Logic
Dependence	Independence

1. Form same-sex small groups. The groups may be unequal in size. Give each small group a sheet of newsprint and a marker, and direct them to list as many positive things about their gender as possible. First caution the teens by saying:

- This is not a contest to see which gender is better; each gender is unique. This is not meant to be other-sex bashing. List things that you feel are true for your sex, but avoid saying negative things such as, "We don't have . . ." or We don't have to . . ." Each group will need a recorder—someone to write down the items on newsprint, and a reporter—someone to read the list aloud. Let's have the person in each group whose first name is the longest be our recorder, and the person whose first name is the shortest be our reporter. Any questions?

Allow several minutes for the small groups to create their lists.

2. When the small groups are finished, have the reporters take turns reading off their group's list. As they read off the items, record them on newsprint. If someone mentions something negative, such as the boys saying, "We don't get PMS," remind them of the instructions and don't write the item on the newsprint.

Many stereotypical items may appear. Just list them and then point this out as part of your observations.

Next, say something like this:

- Not everyone will agree with all these statements. Each person is unique, so it is difficult to make statements that are true of *all* women or *all* men. The field of psychology has some information to contribute to this discussion on what qualities are often associated with females or with males.

3. Display the poster you prepared before the retreat on masculine and feminine traits according to Jung. Convey the following information to the group in your own words:

- Psychologist Carl Jung believed that women and men were designed to complement rather than oppose one another. According to Jung, the feminine part of a man's personality is called the anima, and the masculine part of a woman's personality is the animus. Growth toward human wholeness requires the male to access and integrate his anima into his personality, and the female to do the same with her animus. Individuals who are able to appropriately integrate both sets of traits into their personality are considered androgynous.

Many people view androgyny as the goal of a truly nonsexist society. It describes a condition in which the traits of women and men are not rigidly assigned. People are free to be themselves and to express whatever traits are natural to them. They do not have to be overly concerned about role conformity.

4. To conclude this activity, pose the following questions for group discussion:

- How do you feel about Jung's observations of feminine and masculine traits?
- Do you agree or disagree with them? Why?

(Adapted from Ferder and Heagle, *Partnership*, pp. 135–136)

Yin Yang Small-Group Activity (15–20 minutes)

In this activity the teens assess their own male and female qualities in order to better understand complementarity.

Keep the teens in the same-sex small groups that were formed in the previous exercise, or, if the maturity level of your teens is high, you may form small groups composed of both boys and girls.

Give each teen a copy of handout 6–A, "Yin Yang," and a pencil. Then explain the following directions to the whole group:
• You may have seen this figure before. Yin yang is a Chinese symbol of complementarity. Yin stands for the female—the earth and passive qualities, and yang stands for the male—the heavens and active qualities. Think about the yin and yang qualities you possess. On the yin side of your paper, list the feminine qualities you feel you have. On the yang side, list the masculine ones. You may use the qualities from the Jung chart and also the ones we wrote down during the exercise called Male and Female—What's the Difference? Do you have any questions?

Give the teens enough time to complete their handout and share it with the other members of their small group.

Conclude the activity by leading a large-group discussion of the following questions (see the introduction for alternative ways of debriefing this and other retreat activities):
• Is it possible for one person to have a mixture of both male and female characteristics (for example, intuitive and logical, dependent and independent)? Why or why not?
• Are there any qualities associated with your gender that you do not think fit you?
• Why do you think God made two different genders?
• What do you think God's attitude toward men is? toward women?
• What are some of the good things about the differences between the sexes?

Break (10 minutes)

Defining Sexuality **Large-Group Activity (15 minutes)**
The purpose of this activity is to clarify for the teens the difference between the words *sex* and *sexuality*.

Before the retreat, write the following definitions on poster board or newsprint:
• *Sexual identity.* Our own personal understanding of what it means to be masculine or feminine
• *Sexual orientation.* Who we are attracted to
• *Sexual behavior.* How we express our sexuality in relationships with members of both genders
• *Sexual values.* What we believe is right and wrong, acceptable and unacceptable, permitted and not permitted regarding sex and sexuality

1. Tell the teens to arrange their chairs in a large circle. Distribute a 3-by-5-inch index card and a pencil to each teen. Direct the teens to write an answer to the following question on their card:
• When was the last time you expressed your sexuality? How did you express it?
Assure the teens that their answers will remain anonymous. When they are finished, collect the cards.

2. Next, ask the teens to explain the difference between sex and sexuality. Elicit several responses. Then offer this explanation in your own words:

- Sex is one part of our sexuality just as dessert is one part of a meal. Dessert may taste great, but it alone won't give you the nourishment you need to be healthy. Similarly, sex alone won't create healthy relationships. Sometimes people confuse sex with sexuality, which is a much broader concept. The word *sex* has two different meanings. It can refer to our gender—our sex is either male or female. Or it can refer to the sex act—intercourse. Sexuality includes a wider perspective of who we are. Sexuality can be divided into the following four areas.

Hang up the poster containing the definitions of sexuality that you prepared before the retreat. Briefly explain the definitions to the group. Ask if there are any questions.

3. Read several of the responses from the index cards you collected. You most likely will have a wide range of answers. Conclude the activity with words similar to the following:

- Our sexuality is expressed through all that we do, whether its dressing in a particular way, participating in a group in a certain fashion, or being a loyal friend. Our gift of sexuality is present in each of these situations.

  (Adapted from Parolini, ed., *Sex: A Christian Perspective,* p. 15)

Attitudes

Small-Group Brainstorming (10 minutes)
In this activity the retreatants identify influences on their sexual values.

Have the teens return to their small groups. Then pose this question:

- Where do we get our attitudes regarding sex and sexuality?

  Give the teens these directions, stated in your own words:

- In your small group, discuss this question and decide on the top three influences on our attitudes regarding sex and sexuality. Each group will need a reporter to inform the whole group of your small group's answers. Let's have the oldest person in each group be the reporter. Any questions?

  Give the small groups time to discuss the question. Then have the reporters share their small group's responses. Follow up by asking this question:

- Are these the things you really want to influence your attitudes toward sex and sexuality?

  Offer this conclusion to the activity:

- It is important for us to decide which types of influences we will allow ourselves to be open to. God desires the best for us and for our relationships. We must make sure we are aware of God's presence in our life to balance out the numerous negative voices we hear from society.

Intimate Couples

Small-Group Role-Plays (30 minutes)
In this activity the teens come up with a definition of intimacy and, through role-playing, learn to appreciate the value of intimacy in relationships.

Before the retreat, prepare a poster by drawing a large circle. Write the words *romance, disillusionment,* and *joy* around the outside of the circle, drawing arrows from one to the other.

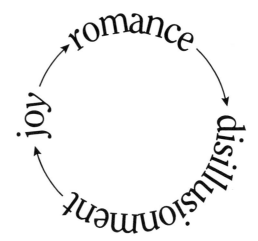

1. Give each small group a copy of a TV guide. Offer these instructions:
*   Choose a TV show that portrays an intimate (or close) couple. Then role-play a scene that might occur on that show—for example, Dr. Quinn; her husband, Sully; and the kids talking as they eat dinner. Each person in the small group must participate in the role-play. At the end of each role-play, the whole group will try to guess what TV show was being acted out.

2. After each role-play, ask the performing group these questions:
*   Why did you choose the show you did?
*   How did you feel acting out the scene?
*   How would this couple define intimacy?

3. After all the role-plays, pose the following questions to the whole group:
*   Who are the most intimate couples on television?
*   How would you define intimacy?
                    (Based on Woods, "Intimacy With God," p. 66)

4. Present the following information in your own words:
*   Intimacy can be defined as a cycle. All love relationships, even relationships with friends and family members, go through three stages: *Romance* can best be described as that infatuation stage during which we believe the other person can do no wrong, we put her or him on a pedestal, and we can't see any of her or his faults.

    The next stage a relationship goes through is *disillusionment.* Suddenly the very things we were infatuated with in the other person now become something we don't particularly like, or we never noticed that the person did. This is kind of the reality-check stage. We get to see the other person for who he or she is. Most relationships end here because we have this misconception that our relationships are always supposed to be in the romantic stage.

If we hang in there, though, we get to the *joy* stage. This is a balanced stage in which we love and appreciate the person for who she or he is—with both faults and strengths. We are comfortable with each other. We have deep, meaningful conversations. We respect each other and give each other room to grow.

Then the cycle begins again. We become infatuated with our partner. He or she buys us flowers on Valentine's Day. But then he or she does something that drives us crazy, and we are back in the disillusionment stage. And then things balance out again, and pure joy takes over.

Conclude the activity by asking a volunteer to read aloud John 15:7,9–12, which expresses God's deepest desire for each of us—that we be filled with joy.

Lunch (45 minutes)

Icebreakers (15 minutes)

Choose from among the icebreakers offered in part A of the appendix of this book, or use games of your own.

Perfect Mate

Small-Group Activity (15 minutes)

The purpose of this activity is for the teens to realize in a fun way the qualities they are looking for in a mate.

Give each person a copy of handout 6–B, "The Perfect Mate," and a pencil. Instruct the teens using words similar to the following:

- As the handout says, you have thirty dollars to spend on a perfect mate. Choose items adding up to, but not going over, thirty dollars. Then you will have a chance to discuss your choices with the members of your small group.

Allow the teens enough time to complete the handout. Next, say:

- We need someone to begin the discussion. Let's have someone start who hasn't been a leader yet. As the leader, you share first and then make sure everyone in your small group gets a chance to share. Afterward you will report back to the whole group about some of the things your group discussed.

When the groups are finished discussing, invite the leaders to share any insights from their small group.

Conclude the activity by raising the following questions for group discussion:

- Were there any items that everyone in your group picked?
- Did anyone's choices surprise you?
- Were there items not on the list that you would have wanted to choose? If so, what are these items?
- How realistic is it to create the perfect mate?

The Scriptures and Sexuality

Small-Group Activity (15 minutes)

In this activity the teens examine the Scriptures to help them understand sexuality as a gift from God.

Introduce the activity by saying something like this:

- Sometimes we forget, but God is the one who created sex and gave us the gift of our sexuality. Although the Bible is full of warnings about abuses of sexuality, it also has a positive view of sexuality. Your group will look at some examples. For this exercise you will need a reader to read the Scripture passages to your small group, a recorder to write down your group's answers, and a reporter to share aloud what your group discussed. Let's have the reader be the person in each group whose birthday is closest to New Year's Day, the recorder be the person whose birthday is closest to the Fourth of July, and the reporter be the person whose birthday is closest to Halloween.

Distribute a Bible, a sheet of paper, and a pencil to each small group. Assign one of the following Scripture passages to each group:
- Gen. 2:18–24
- Gen. 1:26–28,31
- Song of Songs 1:1–3
- Song of Songs 1:15–17
- Song of Songs 7:1,4–7
- Song of Songs 7:9–12
- Prov. 5:3–8,15–17
- 1 Cor. 6:18–20
- 1 Thess. 4:3–8

Note: If the teens question the passages from the Song of Songs, explain that Song of Songs does not condone sex outside of marriage. It describes the love between a king and a Shulammite woman. Song of Songs follows the couple through their courtship, wedding, and married life. Although they are in love from the beginning, they do not consummate their relationship until after they are married. The term *lover* doesn't mean sexual partner, but rather is an affectionate term like *my love* or *my beloved.*

Have the teens discuss the following questions in their small group:
- What does this passage say about sex or sexuality?
- How does this passage define the purpose of sexuality?

After the small-group discussions, invite the reporters to each read their group's passage aloud and summarize their group's answers. When the reporters are done sharing, discuss this question with the group as a whole:
- Taken together, what do these passages say about sex and sexuality? Does this surprise you? Why or why not?

(Adapted from Parolini, ed., *Sex: A Christian Perspective,* p. 16)

Fact or Feeling? Large-Group Activity (10–15 minutes)

This activity shows the teens that love is more than a feeling; true love is a decision.

1. Have the teens arrange their chairs in a large circle. Call for one volunteer to sit on a chair in the center of the circle. Stand beside the chair and have the volunteer sit with his or her eyes closed. Ask the rest of the group to remain silent while you proceed.

Hold your hand about a foot above the volunteer's head. Snap your fingers and ask the volunteer to tell you after each snap where the sound is coming from—the front, the back, or on top. If you can't snap your fingers, clap or strike a spoon against a glass.

Keep your hand equidistant between the listener's ears, alternating your snaps from front to back to top. Or do a few in the same position to trick the person into thinking you might have moved. Ask the person each time where the sound is coming from. (Normally people have limited success in determining where the sound is coming from.)

2. After the experiment, tell the volunteer to open her or his eyes. With the group's help, reveal to the person where the snaps were coming from. The volunteer probably won't believe you! The experience is deceiving but is fun to watch, too.

Depending on the size of the group, you may want to let other volunteers try it.

3. Ask the volunteer(s) the following questions:
• How did you feel during the experiment?
• How did you feel when you were told you were wrong?
• What does this teach you about trusting your feelings?
• How was your experience similar to those of people who say, "It felt right," or "We felt so much in love"?

4. Next, say something like this:
• Sometimes we can be absolutely convinced by how we feel. Our first volunteer was certain the sound was coming from behind [or in front or on top]. Those decisions were based on perceptions or feelings. Our volunteer went into the decision with his or her eyes closed. When asked why they decided to get married, many people say, "It felt right," or "We felt so much in love."

(Adapted from Parolini, ed., *Is Marriage in Your Future?* p. 31)

5. Continue by conveying this information in your own words:
• God's love for us is a covenant, a steadfast promise. God's love is not based solely on feeling. It's a commitment to our well-being. Despite Adam and Eve's disobedience, God continued to love them. God loves us so much that God gave us Jesus. God's love is unconditional. Unconditional love is a decision to treat another person in a particular way and to live out that decision, regardless of changing feelings or circumstances.

6. Have a volunteer read 1 Cor. 13:4–7. Then conclude the activity by asking the whole group these questions:
• What's the difference between love and lust?
• How can sex hurt another person?
• How is this scriptural definition of love different from our society's definition of love?

Honey, If You Love Me

Large-Group Activity (10 minutes)

In this activity the retreatants experience being pressured. This also sets up the next activity, which discusses ways to resist sexual pressure.

Have the teens sit in a circle. Call for a volunteer to start the game by standing in the center of the circle. Give the following instructions in your own words:

- The object of the game is for the person in the center to get someone of the other sex to smile. He or she does that by going up to someone and asking, "Honey, if you love me, won't you please, please smile?" The asker may kneel, sit on the person's lap, sing, anything but tickle the person. Without smiling, the person approached must say, "Honey, I love you, but I just can't smile." If the person does smile, he or she becomes the new asker.

Continue playing the game for several minutes.

Conclude the activity by communicating these points in your own words:

- At times we all feel pressured into doing things we don't feel ready for or don't feel comfortable doing. Many teens experience sexual pressures. In the next activity, we will explore ways to resist these pressures.

(Adapted from Parolini, ed., *Is Marriage in Your Future?* p. 30)

Sex Stress Strategies

Small-Group Role-Plays (20–30 minutes)

The purpose of this activity is for the retreatants to practice strategies to help them resist possible sexual pressures.

Before the retreat, write the following strategies for resisting sexual pressure on poster board or newsprint.

Strategies for Resisting Sexual Pressure

- Avoid situations that may tempt you.
- Say no. Practice saying no as if you really mean it.
- Stick to your answer, and don't allow anyone to change your mind once you've made it up.
- Evaluate your body language to see what message you may be communicating by your attire and attitude.
- Leave. Remove yourself from the pressure situation. Walk away confidently.
- Establish your sexual standards right now rather than on a date during a moment when emotions may run high. Once you set your standards, stick to them.
- Find friends with similar beliefs, and support one another in your values and decisions.

1. Post the strategies and read them aloud to the whole group. Explain these directions in your own words:

- Each small group is to develop a role-play of a situation in which one or more teens is being pressured to do something sexually that he or she does not want to do. In your role-play, have this person use one or more of the strategies for resisting sexual pressure. Please involve everyone in your role-play. After each role-play, the nonperforming groups will attempt to guess which strategies were implemented by the performing group.

2. Give the small groups time to practice. Then have each small group present its role-play. After each role-play, ask the nonperforming groups:

- What resistance strategies did this group use?

3. Conclude the activity by asking the whole group:
- How useful will these strategies be to you in actual situations?
- What are some other resistance strategies a person could use?

Note: Sometimes at this point in the retreat a teen may mention date rape. It is important to address this issue and remind the teens that it is a crime, that the violator needs to be reported, and that the victim needs support and counseling. Asking for help should be encouraged. Have counseling service references available to give out in case a teen privately asks you for help.

Twenty Ways to Say "I Love You"

Small-Group Activity (10 minutes)
The purpose of this activity is for the retreatants to realize that there are many ways to express their love other than by acts of sex.

Give each small group a piece of newsprint and a marker. Introduce the activity this way:
- There are many ways to say "I love you" besides having sex. These creative ways show the other person that you took the time to think about her or him and plan something special. Elect a recorder and a reporter for this activity. On your newsprint your recorder should write down twenty ways to say "I love you" that do not involve sex. The first team to come up with twenty ways, written legibly, wins. I'll give you the first one: do homework together.

As each small group finishes, check to make sure it has twenty legible items. Then have each reporter bring its newsprint up to the front and read off its list.

Conclude the activity by saying something like this:
- Now you have a wealth of ideas for expressing your affection for another person without having sex.

Many Thanks

Affirmation (15–20 minutes)
The purpose of this activity is for the teens to see themselves through the eyes of their friends.

Tell the teens to sit in a large circle. Place one chair in the center of the circle. Invite a volunteer to sit in the chair in the center.

Offer these directions in your own words:
- Everyone in the large circle gets to say what they would be thankful for if they were the person sitting in the center.

Continue in this fashion until every teen has had a turn in the center.

If your group is too large, or if time is limited, have everyone sit in a circle with no one in the center. Direct one person to start and say what he or she would be thankful for if he or she were the person on his or her left. Then have the next person talk about the person on his or her left, and so on. If time permits, repeat the exercise, but this time go to the right.

Closing Guided Meditation

(20–30 minutes)
Begin the meditation with a progressive muscle relaxation exercise (see part C of the appendix for suggestions). If possible, play soft instrumental background music. Then continue with the following guided meditation. Pause for a few seconds at each ellipsis (. . .).

• Sexuality is a gift from God, a gift to be respected and shared with others. God has created us male and female. Each of us is created in the image of God. Every day we learn more about what it means to be created in God's image, and we try to understand this divine mystery of our creation.

Imagine that you have been transported back in time to first-century Palestine. . . . Jesus of Nazareth is a friend of yours. . . . You've known Jesus for many years. . . . Tonight you've been invited to the home of Lazarus—the one Jesus raised from the dead—for a dinner party in Jesus' honor. . . . The sisters of Lazarus—Martha and Mary—are here too. . . . Martha has served the meal. . . . You, Lazarus, and a few others are sitting at the table listening to Jesus. . . . Jesus is a splendid storyteller. . . . You are totally absorbed in what he is saying. . . . Each story is better than the previous one. . . . Jesus just finished telling the one about Peter falling out of the boat when they were fishing. . . . Everyone is laughing. . . . You are feeling the wonderful contentment of having feasted on a delicious meal in the home of friends. . . .

You hardly noticed Mary slip quietly back into the room. . . . She is carrying a small yet beautiful bottle of perfume. . . . She sits at the feet of Jesus and opens the jar. . . . Smell the magnificent aroma of the perfume. . . . She pours the perfume on the feet of Jesus. . . . Everyone is quiet as she does this. . . . Next, she dries his feet with her long black hair. . . . Jesus looks at her lovingly. . . . He gently strokes her head.

You know all too well the rumors that have been surrounding their relationship for years. . . . But you know the truth as well—Jesus loves Mary, and Mary loves Jesus. . . . They care for each other so much that they would never place the other person in a position that would be harmful. . . . You're not surprised when Judas breaks the silence with his irritating question: "Why was this oil not sold and the money given to the poor?" . . . Jesus replies: "Leave her alone. Let her keep it for the day of my burial. . . . You always have the poor with you, but you do not always have me." . . . Judas leaves in a huff. . . .

Jesus returns to his storytelling. . . . He recalls a wedding that he attended in Cana; he tells of the love that was so evident between the bride and the groom. . . . He was sure that the love this couple shared was capable of producing miracles, miracles that will teach us of the love that God has for each of us. . . . Jesus asks you if you've ever seen the power of love produce a miracle. . . . Tell him about one such experience. [Longer pause.]

The meal is over, and the hour is getting late. . . . People are beginning to leave. . . . Jesus asks you if you'd like to walk home with him. . . . Jesus tells you how great it is to have friends like you who believe in him. . . . He asks you to tell him about some of your friends who believe in you and have taught you about love. [Longer pause.]

Then Jesus asks you what qualities you are most grateful for. . . . What qualities do you have that have helped you to build strong relationships? [Longer pause.] Jesus asks you to tell him what's been happening in your life over these past few months. . . . Now is your opportunity to discuss with him the things you've been struggling with. . . . Spend some time telling him about your life. [Longer pause.] Listen to Jesus' comments. He has a message for you. [Longer pause.]

Jesus wants to know about your hopes for the future. . . . Share with Jesus some dreams you have for your future. [Longer pause.]

You reach the point in your journey where you and Jesus must separate. . . . Jesus says good night and tells you how much he has enjoyed being with you tonight. . . . You ask Jesus to bless you. . . . You long to be more like this man. . . . Jesus places his hand on your head and prays a silent prayer for you. . . . Then you continue on your way. . . . As you walk, you say a prayer of thanks for this time to get to know Jesus better: "Dear Jesus, I've enjoyed listening to you and having you listen to me. Relationships are very important to me, and learning how to make them grow deeper is truly a gift. Help me to always appreciate the people you bring into my life. Thank you for the gift of my sexuality. Thank you for making me who I am. Amen."

When you open your eyes, you will no longer be on the road but back here in this room. When you are ready, slowly open your eyes and come back.

Evaluation

Large Group (5 minutes)

After the guided meditation, direct the teens to reflect in writing on the following questions. Invite them to answer aloud if they feel comfortable doing so.

- If you had only one word to describe today, what word would you pick?
- What is one new thing you learned today, or what is one thing you really liked? (It could be something we did or something someone said.)
- What do you feel God is challenging you to do as a result of this retreat?

Yin Yang

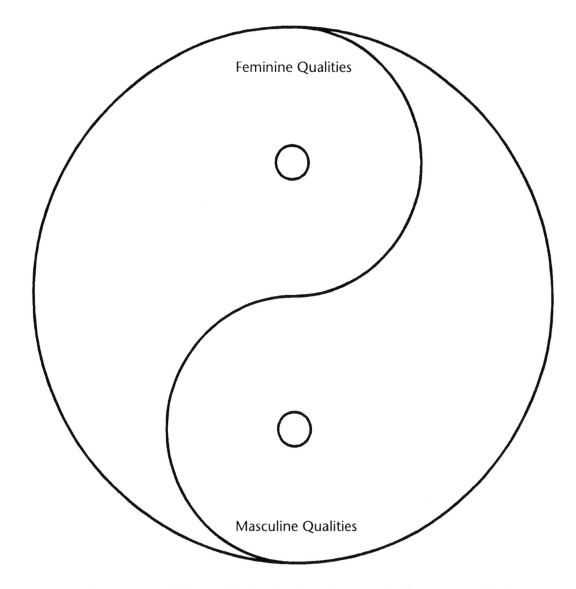

Feminine Qualities

Masculine Qualities

Are there any qualities on the list for the other gender that you would like to develop to become a fuller person? Please list them here.

Handout 6–A: Permission to reproduce this handout for use in your program is granted.

127

The Perfect Mate

You get to create the "perfect mate." You have thirty dollars to spend. Listed below are a number of qualities, each marked with a price. Look over the list and put a check mark next to the qualities you want to purchase with your money.

Attractive body	$6	_____	Good-looking face	$5	_____
Romantic	$3	_____	Good sense of humor	$5	_____
Family oriented	$2	_____	Generous	$4	_____
Great hair	$2	_____	Intelligent	$5	_____
Good manners	$2	_____	Sexy	$4	_____
Good hygiene	$2	_____	Goal oriented	$4	_____
Athletic	$1	_____	Friendly	$4	_____
Tall	$1	_____	Affectionate	$4	_____
Popular	$6	_____	Owns a car	$3	_____
Practicing Christian	$6	_____	Fun	$3	_____
Virgin	$6	_____	Buys presents and cards often	$3	_____
Kind and considerate	$5	_____			
Great kisser	$5	_____	_____ Add your own	$4	_____
Total column 1		_____	Total column 2		_____

Total spent $ _____

Appendix

Part A   Icebreakers

Large-Group Games   Back to Back

Direct everyone to pair off and sit on the floor, back to back. Next, tell them to lock arms and try to stand up together at the same time.

Then have each pair join with another pair and try it again with all four people sitting back to back. When these groups have been successful at standing up, combine larger and larger groups until the entire group is all in one big circle trying to stand up together in the locked-arm, back-to-back position.

(Adapted from Rice, Up Close and Personal, p. 32)

Bob! Bob! Bob!

Have everyone sit in a circle, with the leader standing up in the middle. The leader moves around the circle, randomly pointing at different people. When the leader points at a particular person, the rest of the group should chant that person's name loudly and in rhythm, for example, "Bob! Bob! Bob!" The leader keeps the momentum going by pointing rapidly from one person to another until everyone has been pointed to at least once. The group chants as loudly as possible and claps their hands in time.

(Adapted from Rice, Up Close and Personal, p. 34)

Common Matches

Before the game, write each of the following words on a separate index card:

• Adam	• Eve	• cats	• dogs
• east	• west	• up	• down
• ham	• eggs	• over	• under
• sweet	• sour	• salt	• pepper

Give each person one index card. Make sure there is a match for each person or thing named on a card—for example, Adam and Eve.

When you are ready, invite the teens to mingle around the room and find their "match." When they find that person, have them introduce themselves and wait for further instructions.

After everyone has found their mate, give each pair some scrap paper and a pencil. Tell them they will have 3 minutes to find out and write down things they have in common with their partner (they cannot use such obvious things as two arms, two eyes). They should come up with as many items as possible.

After 3 minutes, go around to each pair and have them share one thing (preferably the most unusual) they have in common.

Group Up

The entire group mingles around the room, and the leader yells out a characteristic, such as "First initial of first name." Everyone must quickly get into groups that share that characteristic (for example, Geri and George would group up). The leader then blows the whistle and identifies the group with the most people in it.

Here are some possible characteristics to use:
- number of people in your immediate family
- month of birth
- favorite color
- color of shirt
- age
- grade in school
- community you live in

(Adapted from Rice and Yaconelli, *Play It!* p. 146)

Lap Game

Direct everyone to stand in a circle shoulder to shoulder, facing in. Next, have them turn to their right, so that they are all facing the same direction. Everyone should be about six inches apart.

On the count of three, tell everyone to sit down gently on the lap of the person behind them. If your group members are really good, they should be able to walk around in a circle while sitting on laps.

(Adapted from LeFevre, *New Games for the Whole Family*, p. 131)

Line Up

Draw two parallel lines on the floor that are about 12 inches apart. Have the whole group line up between the two lines, avoiding standing on the lines.

The object of the game is to reverse the order the teens are standing in *without anyone stepping outside the lines*. It's tough to do without falling, and requires a great deal of cooperation and hanging on to one another.

Next, have the group line up according to birth date, height, or any classification, and the same rules apply. If you have more than one group participating, direct them to compete to see which group can accomplish the switch in the shortest time.

Here is a variation of the game: Line the groups up on a low wall, curb, log, or plank and tell them that the objective is to rearrange the group's order without stepping off the object.

(Adapted from Rice, *Up Close and Personal,* p. 67)

People Upset

The entire group sits in a circle with one less chair than there are people. The extra person stands in the middle. The person in the middle begins by calling out an item or quality that describes people, such as "everyone wearing the color blue." The people who have that characteristic must change chairs with one another. At the same time, the person in the middle also tries to sit down in one of the vacant chairs. The person who fails to secure a chair to sit in is then the caller for the next item or quality. If the person in the center wants everyone to get up, he or she calls out loudly, "People upset," and everyone must move.

Here are the only two rules:
- You can't sit in the chair of the person next to you.
- No diving for chairs is allowed; safety first!

Shared Musical Chairs

This game is played like regular musical chairs except that only a chair is taken away after each round, never a person. The group then has to make sure everyone has a place to sit. The fun and creativity really happens when the number of chairs gets down to three, two, and then one!

Shuffle the Deck

Distribute a playing card to each person. Then call out different combinations, like these:
- Get in a group that adds up to fifty-eight.
- Find three people of the same suit.
- Find five numbers in a row, of any suit.
- Find your whole suit.
- Find four of a kind—four 3s, four 8s, and so on

Direct the teens to form groups based on the combination called. Repeat this several times so that the teens get to meet many people. For larger groups, use multiple decks of cards; for smaller groups, don't use the whole deck. Then create your own combinations.

(Adapted from Rice, *Up Close and Personal,* p. 83)

Virginia Reel

Set up the room before the activity as follows: Place chairs in two rows facing each other. The chairs should be about 18 inches apart. When the teens enter the room, have them sit in any chair. Then give these directions:
- In front of you is your first partner. I will read an open-ended statement and give everyone 1 minute to share their answer with their partner. Then I will say "Rotate," and everyone will then move one chair to the right, facing a new partner. I will then read a new statement for each person to complete.

Here are some possible statements to use (feel free to add your own):

- My favorite color (TV show, movie, book, actor, food, music, animal, season, holiday) is . . . because . . .
- If I could be someone else in my family, I would be . . .
- If I could marry someone famous, I would marry . . .
- If I could invent something, I would invent . . .
- When I have free time, I like to . . .
- Some things I enjoy doing with friends are . . .
- Some things I enjoy doing by myself are . . .
- The world problem I am most concerned about is . . .
- The qualities I look for in a friend are . . .
- Three words that describe me are . . .
- If I could leave anything in my will to my friends, I would leave . . .
- I think the most difficult thing Christ told us to do is . . .
- For breakfast I usually . . .
- The most beautiful thing that I have ever seen is . . .
- A person who's taught me a lot is . . . because . . .
- A time I felt proud was . . .
- A birthday or holiday I'll always remember is . . .

Small-Group Games

Backward Letter Scramble

Ahead of time, make four sets of cards (one set per team), each set containing one of each of the letters *B, A, C, K, W, A, R,* and *D.*

Pass out the cards and have each team member hold one or more cards, depending on how many members are on each team.

Call out a word made up of letters from the cards (for example, card, raw, bark, crab). Direct the players holding the needed letters to line up with their letters, spelling the named word backward. The first team to do so wins.

(Adapted from Rice and Yaconelli, comps.,
Creative Activities for Small Youth Groups, pp. 81–82)

Balloons and Backs

You will need two chairs. Form two teams. Tell the retreatants on each team to divide into trios. If there's an uneven number of people, then some people will have to go twice to even out the trios.

Give each team a balloon and say:
- Stand back to back and lock arms with the other members of your trio.

Place the balloon between their backs and say:
- You must get to the chair at the other end of the room and back without the balloon getting away. Then pass the balloon to the next trio, and the race continues. If the balloon escapes, your team is out of the race. The first team finished wins.

(Adapted from Mike Gillespie, *Jr. High Ministry,* February–March 1996,
"Bountiful Balloon Fun," p. 28. Reprinted by permission from
Jr. High Ministry Magazine, copyright © 1996 by Group Publishing,
P.O. Box 481, Loveland, CO 80539.)

Body Balloon Burst

Secretly and randomly assign each person one of these body parts: right hand, left hand, right foot, left foot, mouth, rear end. There is a corresponding motion for each part of the body:
- "Right hands" raise and wave their right hands.
- "Left hands" raise and wave their left hands.
- "Right feet" hop on their right feet.
- "Left feet" hop on their left feet.
- "Mouths" yell.
- "Rear ends" do the Twist.

When the signal to go is given, each person performs the motion for his or her part of the body in an attempt to attract other body parts and form a complete, six-person "body." No other talking is allowed during this part of the game. Each body must include all six body parts.

When the body is together, the two feet carry one of the hands to the leader, who gives the hand a balloon. The hand (still being carried by the feet) takes the balloon back to its body group where the mouth must blow up the balloon. But the mouth cannot touch it—the hands must hold it for the mouth. After the mouth blows it up, the hands tie it and place it on a chair—at which time the rear end sits on it and pops it. The first team to pop its balloon is the winner.

(Adapted from Rice, *Up Close and Personal,* p. 34)

Connect-a-Name

You will need pieces of newsprint and magic markers. Form teams of four to six people each. For round one, direct the teams, when you give the signal, to each attempt to connect every team member's first name in one crossword puzzle (see diagram below) in the shortest amount of time. Give the signal "Go" for them to begin.

For round two, combine two teams and play again. Continue playing rounds until all players are in one big team making a crossword puzzle of all the names. Display the final crossword during a Bible study on 1 Corinthians, chapter 12, to illustrate that all Christians are part of the same body.

(Adapted from Rice and Yaconelli, *Play It Again!* p. 168)

Knots

If your group is larger than ten, divide into groups of ten or fewer. Each group stands in a circle, and all group members grab one another's hands in the center so that there is a knot of hands at the hub of each circle. Both right and left hands should be connected with someone else.

The two rules are these:

1. You cannot hold hands with the person standing to your right or left.
2. You cannot connect both your hands with the same person.

The object of the game is to untangle the knot without letting go of hands—that is, to unravel arms so that group members end up still in a circle, but holding hands with people to the left and right of them, not in a knot in the middle. Grips can be adjusted, but no letting go.

(Adapted from Rice, *Up Close and Personal*, pp. 64–65)

Kooky Kickball

Like regular kickball, one team is up to bat and the other is in the field.

The first batter kicks the ball as it is rolled to him or her by the other team. A miss, foul, or ball caught in the air is an out. There are three outs per team per inning. If no outs are made, everyone on the team may go up once during the inning. Then the other team goes up to bat.

When the ball is kicked, the fielding team lines up behind the fielder who retrieved the ball. The ball is passed between the legs of all players from front to back. The last team member then takes the ball and tags the runner.

Meanwhile, the kickers (batters) do not run around the bases. Instead, the team that is up to bat lines up single file behind the batter, who runs around the team as many times as possible. One run is scored for every complete revolution before the batter is tagged with the ball.

(Adapted from Rice and Yaconelli, *Play It!* p. 29)

Labels

This game is a form of charades. Everyone in the small group gets a label taped on their back. One at a time, everyone shows their back to the other members of their small group, who have to act out what's on the person's back until he or she guesses correctly. Then the next person in the small group goes. The pattern continues until everyone has gone.

Here are some possible suggestions for labels: Christmas, horse, doctor, baseball, guitar, surfboard, monkey, skateboard, kitten, Fourth of July, merry-go-round, dentist, alligator, football, piano, roller coaster, bicycle, dog, basketball, Thanksgiving, secretary, drums, car, eye doctor, tennis, fish, Easter, trumpet, train, Saint Patrick's Day, Ping-Pong, vacuum cleaner, elephant, teapot, toaster, clock, blender, spaghetti, cook, soccer, tuba, soup, rabbit, volleyball, harp, carpenter, pizza, Valentine's Day, hamburger, dragon, popcorn, hockey, water, Easter egg, Christmas tree, bear, computer, clown, principal, God, church, Bible, giraffe, mechanic, Santa Claus, pancakes, Nintendo.

Name Anagram

On scrap paper, have one person write each group member's first name across the top of the page. Using only those letters, the group must come up with as many words of three letters or more that they can. The team with the most number of words wins.

Popcorn

Prepare bags of popcorn ahead of time. Give one bag to each small group. Invite everyone to take as much popcorn as they want, but tell them not to eat it until instructed.

When everyone has their popcorn, explain, "For each piece of popcorn you took, you have to say one thing about yourself." More than likely the teens will have a pile of popcorn in their lap, and therefore the retreatants will learn a lot about one another.

Shoe Shuffle

If you're a jigsaw puzzle fan, you will love this one. The teens will assemble giant puzzles with their feet. You will need four large sheets of heavy-duty corrugated cardboard, two yards of wide elastic, and a utility knife. (We used a 4-by-8-foot piece of plywood and cord.)

Cut each sheet of cardboard into eight (we did sixteen) jigsaw puzzle pieces approximately 1-foot square. Punch two holes 4 inches apart in the center of each puzzle piece. Thread a piece of elastic through the holes to make a handle, tying a knot on each end to keep it from slipping through the holes.

Divide the teens into four small groups. Give each small group the puzzle pieces for one full puzzle. Be sure that each teen has one or two puzzle pieces. Ask the teens to strap the puzzle piece or pieces to their feet. Then instruct each small group to assemble its puzzle on the floor, using only their feet. No hands are allowed. Tell them that they may begin when you give the signal. Then shout "Go." The first team to construct its puzzle wins.

Scavenger Hunt Relay

Form the retreatants into small groups. Have each small group choose a "runner" for this activity. Ask everyone to get out their purse or wallet. Instruct the whole group by saying something like this:

- I am on a scavenger hunt and need many different items. Some of these items you may have in your purse or wallet. In a moment I will call out the item I need. You must then give the item called for to your runner, who must bring it to me. The first runner to reach me will score one point for his or her team.

    Here is a list of items you may want to request: a penny, a stamp, a driver's license, a calendar, a stick of gum, a picture of a relative, a Band-Aid, a rubber band, matches, a key, a letter, a student ID card, a comb, a pin, a nail file, a hair scrunchie or barrette, a shoelace, a ring, a watch, a social security card, a library card, lip balm or lipstick, jewelry, a sock, sunglasses, exactly forty-one cents, a name tag, an unused tissue.

Short Fuse

You will need one pair of *huge* boxer shorts for every team of three to six young people. You can make them by folding an old sheet in half, cutting it in half, cutting out the legs, and sewing the seams.

Lay the boxer shorts at one end of the room with half the members of each team. Put the other half of each team on the opposite side of the room. Give the whole group these instructions:

• On "Go," the first person in each team quickly puts on the shorts, gathering the shorts around her or him as well as possible, runs to the other side of the room, and tags another team member who hops inside the shorts with her or him. The two of them run back to the other side, make room for another team member, and so on. Continue until all the team members have squeezed into the pair of boxer shorts and have run the relay.

(Michael Capps, "Wacky Ways to Form Groups," *Jr. High Ministry,* November–December 1990, p. 32. Reprinted by permission from *Jr. High Ministry* Magazine, copyright © 1993 by Group Publishing, P.O. Box 481, Loveland, CO 80539.)

Sing-Along

Give each small group a piece of paper and a pencil. Offer these directions:

• You will have 3 minutes to write down on your piece of paper the titles of songs of which each member of your small group can sing at least eight words. Write down as many song titles as possible. Once time is called, you will not be allowed to write down any more titles.

Call time after 3 minutes. Continue with the following directions:

• This is an elimination game. The last small group left with a song to sing wins. When I point to a small group, that group has 3 seconds to begin singing eight words to a song. If other groups have that same song on their list, they must cross it out. There are two ways to be eliminated:

1. If your group sings a song that has already been sung before.
2. When you have no more songs to sing.

Play the game, pointing to various small groups until you have a winner.

Ski Team Relay

Make some skis out of plywood that will accommodate several team members at once. The skis should be approximately four feet long and six inches wide. Use thick plywood that will not break easily. Drill holes in the plywood and put rope through the holes, forming loops for the players' feet. Have each team then race around a goal on these skis.

Staying Put

Give each small group a large piece of newsprint and these instructions:

• Every member of your small group must stand on the newsprint. There may not be any part of anyone's feet hanging over the paper.

When they have done this successfully, instruct the groups to fold the paper in half and give them the same instructions. Once more, have them fold the newsprint in half and see how many groups can have all their members standing on the paper.

Part B   Guided Meditation Tips

- *Read slowly.* Pauses are written into the text for quiet reflection. Do not rush through the text.
- *Read with a little inflection.* A very dramatic reading can be its own distraction. Read beyond a monotone, but try to keep your tone relaxing and conducive to prayer.
- *Read with a rhythm.* After familiarizing yourself with a specific meditation you have chosen, you will recognize its natural rhythm. Flow with that rhythm.
- *Read with confidence.* Before you begin, remind yourself that the Holy Spirit is an active presence. The teens are always in the gentle hands of the Lord during prayer. God will accomplish so much more than any words written or spoken on God's behalf. Be confident in your role as reader and in the role of the Holy Spirit.
- *Find a sacred space.* The location for prayer is often as important as the prayer itself. A sacred environment seems to frame the meditation with an immediate presence of God. Moving to a new location at the outset can create a sense that what follows is different, special, and set aside from everything else. It is important to find an area free from visual distractions. Dimming the lights can also help to create a conducive atmosphere.
- *Listen to the silence.* We are often afraid of silence, hiding from it with radios, televisions, and sound systems. When silence is forced upon us, it is often broken with nervous laughter, whispering, or countless other distractions. Teens are usually uncomfortable at the beginning of the progressive muscle relaxation exercise and then calm down enough to meditate. We usually tell them that we expect some giggling, but that they should try to calm down and enjoy the experience. If any teens are extremely uncomfortable, they may pass, or we may remove them from the room so that they do not distract the others.
- *Use music.* Meditation requires quiet, but soft instrumental music can be used to block unwanted noises and center the teens.
- *Give each person enough space.* Separate the teens as much as possible. We have each teen take his or her own pew or, at most, two teens per pew and have them sit on opposite ends. This not only helps them to get into the meditation but also avoids teens distracting one another.

(Adapted from Catucci, *Time with Jesus*, pp. 10–11)

Part C   Muscle Relaxation Exercises

Have the teens sit or lie down in a comfortable position, legs uncrossed and arms at their sides or loose in front of them. Encourage them to close their eyes or stare at something like a candle or piece of stained glass. Remind them that this is not an exercise to get them to fall asleep. Their bodies are at rest, but their minds should be active.

Tense and Relax • Make a fist with your right hand and tighten the muscles. Then let it go, relax it. Do the same with your other hand. Then make a fist with both hands at the same time. Then relax them.
• Now tighten your whole body. Stretch both arms out, away from your body. Then relax; let your arms flop back down at your sides. Do this a couple of times.
• Shrug your shoulders up high, toward your ears. Then let them drop back down and relax. Do this twice.
• Roll your head around in a circle, slowly. Feel your neck muscles loosen up.
• Press your lips together. Then loosen them.
• Now fill your lungs with air. Breathe in, hold your breath for a few seconds, then breathe out.
• Pull your stomach in. Make it hard and feel your stomach muscles tighten. Now let go and let them relax.
• Arch your back, making it hollow behind you. Then relax.
• Now tighten your leg muscles. First point your toes away from you. Stretch your legs out away from you. Feel the tension in your leg muscles. Then stop pointing and let them relax. Second, bend your feet at the ankles with your toes pointing toward your head. Feel the tight muscles. Now let them relax. Let your feet and your legs relax.
• Take a few more deep breaths without tensing your muscles. Relax for a few moments. How do your muscles feel now? How do you feel?
(Adapted from Youngs, *Stress in Children,* pp. 119–120)

Number Progression • *Picture the number 1,* . . . and feel your legs relax. . . . Feel the clothing around your legs . . . the shoes on your feet . . . your legs pressed against the floor or seat. . . . As the number 1 begins to fade . . . feel the last bit of tension leave your body by moving from your thighs, . . . down through your knees, . . . your calves, . . . your ankles, . . . and now out the bottom of your feet. . . . Your legs are now completely relaxed. . . .

Picture the number 2, . . . and feel your arms and hands relax. . . . Feel the clothing around your arms, . . . any jewelry around your wrists or fingers, . . . your arms against the floor or seat. . . . As the number 2 begins to fade . . . feel the last bit of tension leave your body by moving down from your shoulders, . . . through your upper arms, . . . your elbows, . . . your lower arms, . . . your wrists, . . . and now out your fingertips. . . . Your arms are now completely relaxed. . . .

Picture the number 3, . . . and feel your chest and stomach relax. . . . Be aware of your breathing. . . . Slow your breathing down. . . . Feel your back against the floor or seat. . . . As the number 3 begins to fade . . . feel any weight on your chest begin to rise, . . . making it easier for you to breathe more deeply and slowly. . . . Now your chest and stomach are completely relaxed. . . .

Picture the number 4, . . . and feel your neck and head relax. . . . Think about and then relax your mouth, . . . your cheekbones, . . . your eyes, . . . your forehead. . . . And as the number 4 begins to fade . . . feel the last bit of stress and tension come up from your neck . . . travel through your lower face, . . . through your eyes, . . . your forehead, . . . and out the top of your head. . . .

Your whole body is now completely relaxed. . . . Take another breath in very slowly and deeply.

Floating on Grace • Slowly close your eyes, . . . and feel the stillness. . . . Become part of the quiet. . . . Enter into the silence . . . and become part of it. . . . Rest . . . peacefully . . . silently. . . .

With your eyes closed . . . drift to a place far away. . . . Drift in your imagination . . . to a large body of water . . . a gentle body of water . . . that laps the shore lazily . . . slowly lapping . . . and lapping . . . the water slowly rising . . . and sliding across the shore . . . then withdrawing . . . and sliding back. . . .

Look at the ripples of the surface . . . moving so slowly . . . so gently. . . . Now slowly take a small step forward. . . . Put your foot into the water. . . . It almost tickles, . . . but there is no sense of it being cold. . . . And it has no feeling of being warm. . . . It's the same temperature as you. . . .

And with another small step . . . you realize that it really isn't water . . . it's thicker . . . and it conforms to you. . . . It seems to hold you up . . . making you feel lighter. . . .

Another step . . . slowly . . . and you're up to your knees. . . . It feels dry . . . and buoyant . . . but it still moves and sparkles like water . . . still lapping near the shore, . . . and there is a great feeling of peace . . . and solitude . . . and comfort . . . comfort.

Take yet another step . . . and another . . . until you're up to your waist. . . . You feel incredibly buoyant . . . almost weight-less . . . like a balloon . . . slowly gliding into the sea. . . .

With great courage . . . you let go . . . slowly lean down . . . and push off . . . as if you would swim. . . . It seems impos-sible to sink. . . . You feel as if something is holding you up . . . like a bubble. . . .

You roll over on your back . . . look up into blueness. . . . With no effort . . . you float . . . and feel very light . . . almost suspended. . . .

You close your eyes . . . and drift . . . slowly drift . . . as it laps against you so gently. . . . You feel it slowly melting away the pressures, . . . the tensions, . . . the worries. . . . Drifting . . . slowly . . . relaxed, . . . carefree, . . . and weightless.

(Adapted from Catucci, *Time with Jesus,* pp. 23–24)

Part D Tips for Small-Group Facilitators

We have found that senior high students get more out of a retreat if small-group facilitators are enlisted to help. The role of the facilitator is to help the small group carry out the directions that the retreat leader gives them. The following are guidelines for carrying out this role:

- *Affirm.* Give each teenager genuine compliments when possible.
- *Guide.* When behavior is inappropriate, remind the group of any retreat standards that have been explained and posted at the beginning of the retreat. The following are common retreat standards:
  - ○ What's said here, stays here.
  - ○ Only one person speaks at a time.
  - ○ Put-downs, both verbal and physical, are off-limits.
  - ○ Questions are welcomed.
  - ○ You may decline when invited to share.
  - ○ Be open and try.
- *Encourage.* Try to involve all teenagers in every activity.
- *Respect.* Treat the comments and opinions of all teenagers equally.
- *Share.* See yourself as a member of the group, and do not dominate.
- *Listen.* Make sure everyone has a chance to speak. Show through your body language and verbal comments that the speaker has been heard.
- *Question.* Use questions and comments such as these: "What do the rest of you think?" or "Good comment. Who has something to add?" If a teenager says something off the wall, instead of rejecting the comment, say: "That's not exactly what I expected. Would you like to try again?"

Acknowledgments *(continued)*

The scriptural quotes in this book cited as "Adapted from" are freely adapted and are not to be understood or used as official translations of the Scriptures.

The statistic on page 7 is from an article by David Balsiger, *Group,* February 1995, page 16.

Pick Your Corner on pages 19–20 and Universal Quality on page 20 are based on *Creative Conflict Resolution: More Than Two Hundred Activities for Keeping Peace in the Classroom,* by William J. Kreidler (Glenview, IL: Scott, Foresman and Company, 1984), pages 162 and 156. Copyright © 1984 by William J. Kreidler.

Gift Giving on pages 20–22 is adapted from *Rich World, Poor World: A Curriculum Resource on Youth and Development,* by Alyson Huntly (Dubuque, IA: William C. Brown, 1987), pages 219, 223. Copyright © 1987 by Brown-ROA, a division of Harcourt Brace and Company. Reprinted by permission of Harcourt Brace and Company.

Can I Get In? on pages 23–24 is adapted from *Open Minds to Equality: A Sourcebook of Learning Activities to Promote Race, Sex, Class, and Age Equity,* by Nancy Schniedewind and Ellen Davidson (Englewood Cliffs, NJ: Prentice-Hall, 1983), pages 139–140. Copyright © 1983 by Allyn and Bacon. Used with permission.

Billings' Victory Over Hate on page 25 is adapted from "Billings' Victory Over Hate," by Leslie Ansley, *USA Weekend,* 17–19 March 1995, page 20.

Diversify Yourself on pages 26–27 is adapted from Club Connect, Race Relations Kit, Detroit Public Television. Used with permission.

What Others Think of Me on pages 27–28, Back to Back on page 129, Bob! Bob! Bob! on page 129, Line Up on pages 130, Shuffle the Deck on page 131, Body Balloon Burst on page 133, and Knots on pages 133–134 are adapted from *Up Close and Personal: How to Build Community in Your Youth Group,* by Wayne Rice (El Cajon, CA: Youth Specialties, 1989), pages 91, 32, 34, 67, 83, 34, and 64–65, respectively. Copyright © 1989 by Youth Specialties, 1224 Greenfield Drive, El Cajon, CA 92091. Used by permission of Zondervan Publishing House.

The information about the Book of Joshua on page 35, the quote from Psalm 16 on handout 4–E, and the information about Samuel on pages 100–101 are adapted from the Youth Bible, New Century Version (Dallas: Word Publishing, 1991), pages 194–195, 489–490, and 244–245, respectively. Copyright © 1991 by Word Publishing. Used with permission. All rights reserved.

The graduation prayer, by Jim Dinn, on handout 2–I is from *The Fire of Peace: A Prayer Book,* compiled and edited by Mary Lou Kownacki, OSB (Erie, PA: Pax Christi USA, 1992), pages 64–65. Copyright © 1992 by Pax Christi USA. Used with permission.

The statistics about hunger and poverty on page 64 are from *Bread for the World Annual Report 1995* and *The State of America's Children Yearbook 1995,* by the Children's Defense Fund, Washington, D.C.

The divorce statistics on page 64 are from the Women's Legal Defense Fund, University of Denver, U.S. Census Bureau, National Center for Health Statistics, as reprinted from *Youthworker Update,* October 1995, page 4.

Jesus Changes Things on page 76 and the material on handout 4–A are adapted from *Good Clean Fun: Fifty More Nifty Games for Your Youth Group,* volume 2, by Tom Finley (Grand Rapids, MI: Zondervan Publishing House, 1988), pages 60 and 61. Copyright © 1988 by Youth Specialties, 1224 Greenfield Drive, El Cajon, CA 92091. Used by permission of Zondervan Publishing House.

The Yurt Circle game on page 77 is adapted from *More New Games! and Playful Ideas from the New Games Foundation,* by Andrew Fluegelman (New York: Doubleday, 1981), page 123. Copyright © 1981 by the Headlands Press.

The Lap Game on page 77 is based on *The New Games Book,* by the New Games Foundation, edited by Andrew Fluegelman (New York: Doubleday, 1976), page 171. Copyright © 1976 by the Headlands Press.

The statistics on prayer on page 79 are from "What Really Impacts Kids' Spiritual Growth," *Group Inside,* February 1995, page 21, and from *What's a Christian?* by Paul Woods (Loveland, CO: Group Publishing, 1990), page 4. Copyright © 1990 by Group Publishing.

The story on page 79 is from "Bringing God into the World, *Newsweek,* 6 January 1992, page 40.

The Power of Prayer on pages 79–81 is based on "The Power of Prayer," by Amy Nappa, *Group Inside,* March–April 1995, page 62; and *Group's Real Life Bible Curriculum: When God Seems Silent,* by Mike Nappa (Loveland, CO: Group Publishing, 1995), n.p. Copyright © 1995 by Group Publishing.

The quotes on resource 4–A are from Nappa, *When God Seems Silent,* n.p. Reprinted by permission from Group Publishing, P.O. Box 481, Loveland, CO 80539.

The material about prayer on page 82 and 84, and the material on handout 4–D is adapted from the Discovering Program student booklet for *Praying,* by Dolores Ready (Winona, MN: Saint Mary's Press, 1989), pages 13, 13–14, and 14, respectively. Copyright © 1989 by Saint Mary's Press. All rights reserved.

Who Would You Choose? on page 99 is adapted from *Get 'Em Talking: 104 Great Discussion Starters for Youth Groups,* by Mike Yaconelli and Scott Koenigsaecker (Grand Rapids, MI: Zondervan Publishing House, 1989), page 93. Copyright © 1989 by Youth Specialties.

The facts about famous people on pages 102–103 are adapted from "Consider This," *Chicken Soup for the Soul: 101 Stories to Open the Heart and Rekindle the Spirit,* by Jack Canfield and Mark Victor Hansen (Deerfield Beach, FL: Health Communications, 1993), pages 228–230. Copyright © 1993 by Jack Canfield and Mark Victor Hansen. Used with permission.

Top That on page 103 is adapted and reprinted with permission from *Group's Active Bible Curriculum: Overcoming Insecurities,* by Carol Younger (Loveland, CO: Group Publishing, 1991), pages 23–24. Copyright © 1991 by Group Publishing, P.O. Box 481, Loveland, CO 80539.

Past Achievements on pages 104–105 is adapted from *Look Who's Drivin' the Bus,* unit 1, session 3, by Roberta Rubly-Burggraff (Milwaukee: HI-TIME Publishing, 1987), pages 5–6. Copyright © 1987 by HI-TIME Publishing, P.O. Box 13337, Milwaukee, WI 53213-0337. Used with permission.

Excerpts from Male and Female on pages 115–116 are adapted from *Partnership: Women and Men in Ministry,* by Fran Ferder and John Heagle (Notre Dame, IN: Ave Maria Press, 1989), pages 135–136. Copyright © 1989 by Ave Maria Press, Notre Dame, IN 46556. Used with permission of the publisher.

Defining Sexuality on pages 117–118 and The Scriptures and Sexuality on pages 120–121 are adapted and reprinted with permission from *Group's Active Bible Curriculum: Sex: A Christian Perspective,* edited by Stephen Parolini (Loveland, CO: Group Publishing, 1990), pages 15 and 16. Copyright © 1990 by Group Publishing, P.O. Box 481, Loveland, CO 80539.

Intimate Couples on pages 118–119 is based on "Ready to Go Meetings: Intimacy with God," by Paul Woods, *Group Inside,* October 1992, page 66.

Fact or Feeling? on pages 121–122 and Honey, If You Love Me on pages 122–123 are adapted and reprinted with permission from *Group's Active Bible Curriculum: Is Marriage in Your Future?* (Loveland, CO: Group Publishing, 1990), pages 31 and 30. Copyright © 1990 by Group Publishing, P.O. Box 481, Loveland, CO 80539.

Group Up on page 130 and Kooky Kickball on page 134 are adapted from *Play It! Over Four Hundred Great Games for Groups,* by Wayne Rice and Mike Yaconelli (Grand Rapids, MI: Zondervan Publishing House, 1986), pages 146 and 29. Copyright © 1986 by Youth Specialties. Used by permission of Zondervan Publishing House.

Lap Game on page 130 is adapted from *New Games for the Whole Family,* by Dale N. LeFevre (New York: Perigee Books, 1988), page 131. Copyright © 1988 by Dale N. LeFevre. Used by permission of the Berkley Publishing Group. All rights reserved.

Backward Letter Scramble on page 132 is adapted from *Creative Activities for Small Youth Groups,* compiled by Wayne Rice and Mike Yaconelli (Winona, MN: Saint Mary's Press, 1991), pages 81–82. Copyright © 1991 by Youth Specialties, 1224 Greenfield Drive, El Cajon, CA 92021. Used by permission.

Connect-a-Name on page 133 is adapted from *Play It Again! More Great Games for Groups,* by Wayne Rice and Mike Yaconelli (Grand Rapids, MI: Zondervan Publishing House, 1993), page 168. Copyright © 1993 by Youth Specialties. Used by permission of Zondervan Publishing House.

The guided meditation tips on page 137 and the muscle relaxation exercise Floating on Grace on page 139 are adapted from *Time with Jesus: Twenty Guided Meditations for Youth,* by Thomas F. Catucci (Notre Dame, IN: Ave Maria Press, 1993), pages 10–11 and 23–24. Copyright © 1993 by Ave Maria Press, Notre Dame, IN 46556. Used with permission of the publisher.

The muscle relaxation exercise Tense and Relax on page 138 is adapted from *Stress in Children: How to Recognize, Avoid, and Overcome It,* by Dr. Bettie B. Youngs (New York: Arbor House, 1985), pages 119–120. Copyright © 1985 by Arbor House.